D1713945

Reading and Interpreting the Works of

GEORGE ORWELL

Enslow Publishing
101 W. 23rd Street
Suite 240
New York, NY 10011
USA
enslow.com

Lit Crit Guides

Reading and Interpreting the Works of

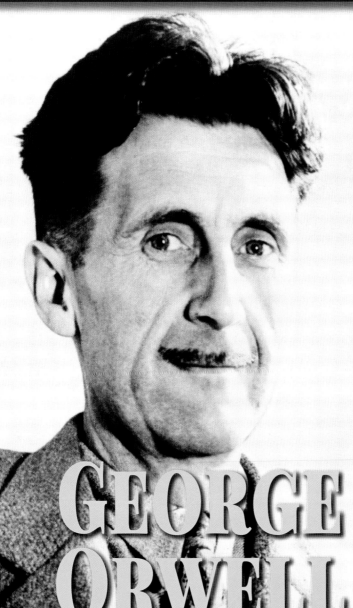

GEORGE ORWELL

Audrey Borus

For Andrea: who brought that important book in the nick of time

Published in 2017 by Enslow Publishing, LLC
101 W. 23rd Street, Suite 240, New York, NY 10011

Library of Congress Cataloging-in-Publication Data

Names: Borus, Audrey, author.
Title: Reading and interpreting the works of George Orwell / Audrey Borus.
Description: New York, NY : Enslow Publishing, 2017. | Series: Lit crit guides | Includes bibliographical references and index.
Identifiers: LCCN 2016026256 | ISBN 9780766083547 (library bound)
Subjects: LCSH: Orwell, George, 1903-1950—Criticism and interpretation—Juvenile literature.
Classification: LCC PR6029.R8 Z58927 2016 | DDC 828/.91209—dc23
LC record available at https://lccn.loc.gov/2016026256

Printed in Malaysia

To Our Readers: We have done our best to make sure all website addresses in this book were active and appropriate when we went to press. However, the author and the publisher have no control over and assume no liability for the material available on those websites or on any websites they may link to. Any comments or suggestions can be sent by e-mail to customerservice@enslow.com.

CONTENTS

George Orwell

"Prose Like a Window Pane"

The man who would become George Orwell knew at an early age he was destined to be a writer because to be anything else was "outraging my true nature."[1] By his own reckoning, Orwell started writing when he was young, partly because he was isolated and unpopular: "I had the lonely child's habit of making up stories and holding conversations with imaginary persons, and I think from the very start my literary ambitions were mixed up with the feeling of being isolated and undervalued."[2] Later, Orwell wrote for political reasons as well, and though he has been dead for more than sixty years, he "continues to generate keen interest and intense debate both within the literary academy and in the public at large."[3] The combined sales of Orwell's last two novels (*Animal Farm* and *Nineteen Eighty-Four*) total more than fifty million copies and have become required reading in high schools and colleges around the world.

In his essay "Why I Write," Orwell suggested that every writer is motivated by four drives:

> i. Sheer egoism—Desire to seem clever, to be talked about . . .

> ii. Aesthetic enthusiasm—Perception of beauty in the external world . . .

iii. Historical impulse—Desire to see things as they are, to find out true facts . . . iv. Political purpose—Desire to push the world in a certain direction . . .[4]

In total, he produced six long novels and countless essays, journals, and political writing. He felt that when he lacked political purpose, he wrote "lifeless books and was betrayed into writing purple passages, sentences without meaning, decorative adjectives and humbug generally."[5] "Good prose," Orwell wrote, "is like a window pane": clear, concise, and completely transparent.[6]

aesthetic

Perception of beauty

Today, every one of Orwell's books is available in print in English. The twenty-two volumes of *The Complete Works of George Orwell*, edited by Peter Davison, are currently available in cloth-bound and paperback editions.[7] Orwell was a prolific writer who drove himself, often doubting whether he was good enough, then questioning the value of being good. "Orwell was a private man and the thought of a biographer digging into his past would not have pleased him," writes biographer Michael Sheldon.[8] Ironically, since 2000, three biographies of Orwell have been published, and according to Orwell scholar John Rodden, he is arguably the "best-known literary figure of the twentieth century."[9]

This book aims to introduce George Orwell to readers and to show how his status as a literary giant was achieved. We will examine how he made accessible to a wide number of readers a genre of literary criticism and political commentary, speaking directly to the reader with a combination of careful observation and meticulous use of language. Readers will explore Orwell's narrative style, which "merges the techniques of journalism and fiction—using the dramatic powers of dialogue, setting and character to strengthen the powers of factual observation and commentary."[10] To that end, we'll take an in-depth look at several of Orwell's essays and the two works for which he is best known: *Animal Farm* and *Nineteen Eighty-Four*.

An Age Like His

George Orwell lived in an interesting era. Though he was only forty-six when he died, his life spanned three wars: World War I, the Spanish Civil War, and World War II. He was born Eric Blair on June 25, 1903, in Motihari, Bengal, India. His father, Richard Blair, was from a middle-class family, though at some point the family had had aristocratic connections. Eric's father was very much a Victorian-era man. Reserved and cautious, he maintained a staid exterior, a "conservative man who liked to keep his life within the confines of an undemanding routine."[1]

By contrast, Eric's mother, Ida Mabel Limouzin, is described as lively and attractive. She was also nearly half her husband's age. The two British citizens met in India where Richard was an assistant sub-deputy opium agent and Ida was a governess. The couple married in 1896. In 1898, their first daughter, Marjorie, was born, and in 1903 Eric came along. Ida and the children moved to Oxfordshire, England, a year later, while her husband stayed in India for the remaining seven years until his retirement. Living apart from family is not as unusual as it may sound, since in those days "the custom was to send English children [of that age] back home to be educated,"[2] and though some mothers remained with their husbands in India, many chose to stay with their children. Still, it couldn't have

Young Eric is held by his mother, Ida, in 1903.

OPIUM TRADE AND THE BRITISH EMPIRE

The Turks and Arabs first introduced opium, made from poppy plants, into China in the sixth or seventh century. Used for pain relief, it was only available in limited quantities. But in the seventeenth century, the drug became widely available and users found that it could be mixed with tobacco and smoked. Because of its addictive and damaging effects, China outlawed its use. But that did not stop the drug from coming into the country.

By the late 1700s, the British had become the leading suppliers of opium. The British East India Company had control over cultivation in Bengal and used its monopoly to sell opium in China. The British did this in an attempt to balance trade with China: the West wanted tea, silk, and porcelain from China, but China did not really want much from Britain or any other European country. To keep trading with China, Western countries had to pay with gold or silver. The opium trade changed that by creating a steady demand from Chinese addicts or by creating new ones.

The East India Company never dealt directly with China because it was illegal. Rather, it licensed private traders to take opium from India to China. The traders then sold the drug to smugglers, who would pay in gold and silver. These were farmed back into China as the East India Company purchased the goods it could sell for profit in England.

By 1907, opium was not nearly as important and China made agreements with India to reduce and finally stop its cultivation. Fortunately, Richard Blair was close to retirement at this point.

done much to foster family relations. Biographers all mention that Ida treated Richard with a certain amount of disdain, and the fact that Eric never really got to know his father was a source of his never-ending quest to gain his approval.

In 1907, Richard Blair came home on leave from India, and in 1908, Eric's younger sister, Avril, was born. For the next four years, Eric, his sisters, and his mother lived in a small town called Henley-on-Thames. In his notebooks and essays, Eric's memories seem pleasant, if a bit idealized, full of summers fishing and time spent outdoors.

All that changed in the fall of 1911, when Eric, then eight, was shipped off to St. Cyprian's, a preparatory school 60 miles (96 kilometers) south of London. Mrs. Blair thought her son had intellectual potential—especially with his talent for words—and was determined to place him at a school that had a track record of sending boys to a top-notch public school (the equivalent of private school in the United States), such as Eton, Westminster, or Harrow. Because the family could not afford the 180-pound yearly tuition, Eric was accepted on scholarship, a fact that he claims the headmaster and his wife later "began throwing in my teeth."[3] As a scholarship boy, he was expected to win prizes and bring credit to the school.

St. Cyprian's was probably not very different from other schools of its time, but for a student like Eric, it was torture. In fact, thirty years later, he would write an essay, "Such, Such Were the Joys," cataloging the snobbery, pretentiousness, and indignities he suffered there. Despite his treatment, Eric excelled academically (though he would later disparage the kind of rote learning the school encouraged as "positive orgies of dates with the keener boys leaping up and down in their places in their eagerness to shout out the right answers and at

A MAN OF ORWELL'S TIME

When young Eric Blair arrived in England in 1904, Queen Victoria had been dead for three years, and her son Edward VII had taken the throne. Like his mother, the new king "defined an age which was one of emancipation, liberalism, social and scientific innovation, and confidence in the future."[4] It was a time when politicians were arguing for state reform such as pensions and national insurance. But it was also a time of great empire building. Great Britain had laid claims to lands on every continent and every terrain.

Eric's family was solidly middle class—not overly rich, but certainly not poor—so it was expected that Eric would be educated. The books, games, and toys of his childhood would have been concerned with soldiers and the glory in fighting World War I. As he got older, his "sexual education was a jumble of misinformation, low jokes, and noble laments for lost love. A boy of his time and social class could not have expected much else."[5]

the same time not feeling the faintest interest in the meaning of the mysterious events they were naming."[6]

Eric won a place at Wellington College, where he stayed for nine weeks before receiving a scholarship to Eton in 1917. His biographer notes that World War I was "merely a series of pointless movements back and forth over ravaged muddy fields."[7] Nonetheless, Eric served in Eton's Officer Training Corps, albeit without much enthusiasm for the drills, inspections, and routine maneuvers the Corps demanded. Academically, Eric did not thrive at Eton. In various biographical accounts, it sounds as if he simply turned off his brain. "After all that ferocious cramming from the Wilkes he had decided to slack off. During his first two or three years, although he failed to distinguish himself, at least he held his place in his Election [class]—not quite bottom."[8]

None of Eric's contemporaries at Eton really got to know him well. According to one classmate, "He had a large, rather fat face, with big jowls, a bit like a hamster and a noticeably croaky voice. His best feature were his 'slightly protruding blue eyes.' Another contemporary called him 'pretty awful [and] a bit of a bastard,' while others noted his aloofness and lack of sympathy."[9] He did have friends, like Steven Runciman, who seemed to understand his "mind worked differently from other boys' and [he] didn't really like other people. 'He liked their intellectual side, but friends didn't really mean anything to him.'"[10] Despite his less than stellar record as a scholar, he was recognized as intelligent, if argumentative. According to biographer Gordon Bowker, he became known as "Socratic, challenging received ideas and drawing others into contentious dialogues."[11]

Unlike his classmates who went on to Oxford and Cambridge, Blair followed in this father's footsteps and joined the Indian Civil Service and became a policeman in Burma (Myanmar), "an unlikely if not unprecedented career choice for an Etonian."[12] After five years, Blair realized that he was not cut out to be a civil servant. In fact, critics believe that his time in Burma contributed to his enduring opposition to anything resembling imperialism. (Imperialism is a way for a country to increase its power by gaining control over countries. The British grew their empire by controlling many countries in the Middle and Far East.) The experience did provide him with ample material to write a novel called *Burmese Days*, as well as powerful essays and short stories such as "A Hanging" and "Shooting an Elephant." In fact, much of Orwell's writing draws from personal experience.

In 1927, he left Burma on medical leave. He had contracted dengue fever, a disease spread by mosquitos that is not fatal but can cause long-lasting fevers and rashes. He was given eight months to recuperate and during this time decided not to return to Burma. Instead, he would devote himself to writing. But it wasn't just that he wanted to be a full-time writer. Serving in Burma had offended him morally. As a "servant of the Empire," he had been unable to think or act freely, and the thought of returning to his old job to "face another long term of silent misery in a world plagued by heat, hypocrisy, loneliness and guilt" was abhorrent.[13] Blair turned in his resignation before his eight months of leave were over, thereby forfeiting not only his yearly salary, but the rest of his sick leave pay. The difficulty was telling his parents, his father in particular. "Eric was rejecting not merely a job but a tradition of selfless service that men such as Mr. Blair had proudly upheld. His decision went against everything that his father stood for, and to make matters worse, he was giving it all up for a vague plan to write books."[14]

Blair wanted to write a book about his experiences, but hadn't really formulated a plan for the scope of that book. He decided to take up tramping in an attempt to gather first-hand information about living rough. This entailed traveling around the English countryside and Paris, pretending to be poor and homeless. But there was another factor in his decision. Biographer Sheldon points out that Blair *needed* to tramp: "He needed to see the poor at close quarters, talking directly with them about their lives, sharing meals with them, sleeping in the same rooms."[15] In his's own words: "I wanted to submerge myself, to get right down among the oppressed, to be one of them and on their side against their tyrants."[16] But Blair did not go as himself. Rather, he adopted the persona of a man who was penniless and uneducated. He called himself P.S. or Edward Burton. According to critics such as Gordon Bowker, this is evidence of Blair's deceptive, almost dishonest nature: "He had shrugged off one role—imperial policeman— and taken on another—that of a man brought down through drink and poverty. As it happened, he had money in the bank and was comparatively abstemious [not drinking much]."[17]

Initially, Blair had been staying with his parents in South-wold. Through friends of his sister, Blair was able to find cheap lodging in London. However, like many aspiring writers of the day, he ended up going to Paris. Though he later explained his going to France was to live cheaply and to teach English if he ran out of money, Bowker suggests that he may have been following a road "trodden by so many writers before him," in particular James Joyce, whose writing Blair very much admired.[18]

From 1928 to 1930, when Blair was in Paris, several of his works were published in France as well as England. His health was not good, and at one point he was hospitalized in a Parisian hospital with pneumonia, an experience he recorded with great horror and clarity in his journals and essays.

Becoming George Orwell

By 1930, Blair was back in England writing articles for the magazine *Adelphi*. One of his first pieces to appear in the magazine was a review of Louis Mumford's biography of Herman Melville. Though not yet using a pseudonym, biographer Michael Sheldon notes this review was "the first published piece in which the distinctive voice of Orwell emerges."[19] All the time he had been gathering notes and experiences for writing, he was also forming political ideology, becoming a "literary man with a sociological eye and a sociological imagination."[20]

In 1933, with the publication of *Down and Out in Paris and London*, Eric Blair took the pen name "George Orwell." Some critics have suggested that he did this to protect his respectable middle-class family, while others see his adopting a pseudonym as evidence that he was deliberately deceptive.[21] Though the book was not a huge success, critics reviewed it favorably and even the popular press gave it positive reviews.

pseudonym

A name taken that is not one's own; an alias.

Meanwhile, Orwell had been teaching at a private school called the Hawthorns in Hayes, a town just outside London. In a letter to an acquaintance dated 1932, Orwell writes:

> I have been teaching at [this] foul place for nearly two months. I don't find the work uninteresting but it is very exhausting & apart from a few reviews, etc I've hardly done a stroke of writing. The most disagreeable thing here is not the job itself (it is a day-school, thank God, so I have nothing to do with the brats out of school hours) but Hayes itself, which is one of the most godforsaken places I have ever struck. The population seems to be entirely made up of clerks who frequent tin-roofed chapels on Sundays & for the rest bolt themselves within doors.[22]

Orwell's intense dislike of Hayes seems to stem from its "dreary uniformity"[23] and the fact that the countryside he loved was being usurped by urban sprawl. In fact, the Hawthorns was owned by a businessman who worked for the gramophone factory in the town. (Orwell did not like the

The Review of Herman Melville's Biography

For the most part, Blair praised Louis Mumford's biography of Herman Melville. He called the book admirable but noted that Mumford's "declared aim to expound, criticize—and unpleasant but necessary word—interpret" was its biggest fault. In fact, Blair remarks that interpretation of a writer's work is "a dangerous method of approaching a work of art" and that interpreting such works is like "eating an apple for the pips."[24] In Blair's view, Mumford is at his best when he "relates Melville to his times, and shows how the changing spirit of the century made and marred him."[25] The review goes on to reveal Blair's notion of what makes a writer—"passionate sensitiveness; to [Melville] seas were deeper and skies vaster than to other men, and similarly beauty was more actual"[26]—as well as his ideas about true freedom and the oppression of industrialism, themes that would later emerge in *Animal Farm* and *Nineteen Eighty-Four*.

phonograph; he saw it as the "emblem of modern decadence, the mindless reproduction of machine-made ideas and dictated opinions."[27])

Though Orwell would leave the school after only a few years, the experience would give him material for his play *A Clergyman's Daughter*, which was published in 1935. In 1936, Orwell's publisher, Victor Gollancz, asked him to write about working conditions in northern England. The result was the book *The Road to Wigan Pier*, which Gollancz included as an offering in his Left Wing Book Club. The book not only brought him to the attention of a larger audience, it also "revealed his talent as an investigative journalist."[28] That same

THE SPANISH CIVIL WAR

In 1934, a revolution divided Spain. Socialists in the country were afraid that, as in Austria and Germany, the government would move to Fascism. The right wing countered that the government was "a prisoner of the revolutionary left."[29] Different parties seized control of different areas of the country. Catalonia and Basque provinces were loyal to the Republican (left-wing) government because they felt it supported their interests and would not interfere with them. Andalusia and Galicia went to the Nationalists (right-wing). In Madrid and Barcelona, the workers defeated the Nationalists. "Thus, in broadest terms, the Republic held the centre, the Levant, Catalonia, and the Basque industrial zones; the Nationalists controlled the food-producing areas, which was to cause an increasingly acute food shortage in the Republican zone."[30]

But factions of the left (Partido Comunista de España [Spanish Communist Party or PCE] and Left Republicans) were not happy about the way events were playing out. Britain and France refused to acknowledge the left-wing government now in power or to sell arms to it. The Soviet Union, on the other hand, supplied arms to the PCE. In the fall of 1936, another left-wing party, the National Confederation of Labour (Confederación Nacional del Trabajo; CNT) was brought into the Popular Front, the larger left-wing party now in control. This caused further fracturing of the left. Then in May 1937, a small Marxist revolutionary party, the Workers' Party of Marxist Unification (Partido Obrero de Unificación Marxista, or POUM), set off a rebellion in Barcelona to demand a workers' government rather than what the Popular Front had formed. It was into this conflict that Orwell arrived.

year Orwell married Eileen O'Shaughnessy, a graduate student working on a master's degree in educational psychology.

In the Lenin Barracks in Barcelona

In 1937, Orwell went to Spain to fight in its civil war. The conflict had been some time in the making. There were so many opposing political factions in Spain "that no political party could cater to all of them. Besides the numerous political parties, ranging from the Communists on the left to the Fascists on the right, there were organizations of workers that wanted to overthrow the government and establish a new economy under the control of the workers."[31] There was also a strong pro-Catholic party opposing those who wanted to abolish the church. On top of that, there were regional and ethnic loyalties, especially among the Basques and the Catalans in the northeastern part of Spain, who wanted autonomy, or self-government. Germany and Italy were sending arms and some troops to aid the Spanish Nationalists. Francisco Franco was their leader, and he had an affinity for Fascism. On the Republican side, aid was coming from the Soviet Union and also from many other foreigners, who were strongly against Fascism, and who signed on to fight. In fact, more than thirty-five thousand fought for a republic in the International Brigades, military units made up of soldiers from other countries.[32]

Orwell joined Partido Obrero de Unificación Marxista (Worker's Party of Marxist Unification), or POUM, who were displeased with the Spanish communists aligned with Soviet leader Joseph Stalin. On May 20, 1937, Orwell suffered a nearly fatal shot in the throat and moved from the Husesca front to a nearby hospital and then to Barcelona. A friend brought his wife, Eileen, to Barcelona for his recuperation. But he could no longer fight—his medical discharge declared him useless—and he did not want to be a war correspondent. What he wanted to do was to get away from it all, "away from the horrible atmosphere of political suspicion and hatred, from streets thronged by armed men, from air-raids, trenches, machine-guns, screaming trams, milkless tea, oil cookery, and shortage of cigarettes—from almost everything that I had learnt to associate with Spain."[33]

In the meanwhile, the government outlawed the POUM, rounding up its leaders and imprisoning and killing them. In fact, Orwell and his wife were at risk, though Orwell could not understand why. It was his wife who pointed out to him that the "ordinary notions of justice did not apply." "It did not matter what I had done or not done. This was not a round-up of criminals; it was merely a reign of terror. I was not guilty of

Orwell poses with POUM militia guards in Barcelona in 1936. (He is the tallest man standing in the back.) A year later he suffered a gunshot wound, ending his involvement in the Spanish Civil War.

Fascism, Communism, and Socialism

Benito Mussolini, Europe's premiere Fascist leader, coined the term "fascism" from the Latin word *fasces*, meaning a bundle of elm or birch rods that was a symbol of punishment in ancient Rome. The philosophy centers around a supreme government, often ruled by a dictator, that everyone must obey and never question. Though there are differences by country, fascist movements share common elements such as extreme militaristic nationalism, contempt for elections, anything that appears to be politically or culturally liberal, and a belief that there is a natural social hierarchy in which elite classes rule, a *Volksgemeinschaft* (in German, "people's community"), in which individual interests are subordinate to the good of the nation.

Communism in the most basic sense is a political system in which the government owns everything: land, businesses, utilities, and so on. In other words, everything is owned in common and is available when needed. Socialism, on the other hand, is the intermediate stage between communism and capitalism. In socialist governments, there is collective ownership of the means of production and distribution of goods.

any definite act, but I was guilty of 'Trotskyism.'"[34] All of these experiences sealed Orwell's "conversion to socialism, while also instilling in him an abiding hatred of Communism—especially the Stalinist version that the POUM had opposed."[35]

Back in England, Orwell could see that communists around the world were distorting events in Spain by saying that the POUM and anyone siding with them were fascists. He tried to correct this by writing *Homage to Catalonia*, an account of his time in Spain, but Victor Gollancz refused to publish it or anything critical of communism. Frederic Warburg did publish it in April of 1938, and the reviews were mixed. At the same time, Orwell was sick with tuberculosis and spent five and half months in a sanatorium. He then went to Morocco to convalesce and work on his next novel, *Coming Up for Air*, which was published in 1939.

A Thorn in the Side of Editorial Complacency

By 1939, Orwell and his wife had returned to England and were living in London. World War II was beginning. Eileen got a job with the Censorship Department, while George tried to enlist in the military, failing because of his poor health. At this point, he began writing essays that were collected into the volume *Inside the Whale*. The essays included critiques of authors ranging from Charles Dickens to Henry Miller, as well as topics such as weekly publications for boys. According to Orwell scholar John Rossi, this collection was "something unique. The essay 'Boys Weeklies,' in particular foreshadowed the new academic genre of cultural studies—a serious essay on a seemingly frivolous subject."[36]

Orwell appears to have been energized by the blitzkriegs (heavy bombings) of April and May 1940. He wrote movie and play reviews for a publication called *Time and Tide* and was writing a series called "London Letters" for the American journal *Partisan Review*—"wide-ranging pieces, covering the current political situation, wartime conditions in England, literary gossip, attitudes toward American soldiers in Britain, and of course, strongly expressed personal opinions about everything."[37]

foreshadow

A literary device used to suggest events that may be coming.

Early in 1941, Orwell published *The Lion and the Unicorn*, in which he argued that a revolutionary movement was emerging in England and its basis was patriotism, a force he saw as far more binding than the alleged solidarity of the working class. He believed that patriotism, at least in England, could be leveraged to form a kind of socialism. But by June of 1941, the moment had passed and Orwell was working for the BBC India Section of the Eastern Service to counter the propaganda the Germans were using to undermine British rule in India. The role of the Indian Section of the Eastern

From 1941 to 1943, Orwell worked at the BBC, producing radio broadcasts to India on the progress of the war.

Service was "to make the voice of Britain heard in India"[38] and reinforce the ties between two countries. However, as Sheldon points out, the job amounted to "a kind of cultural imperialism. So many of the programs that were broadcast to India had nothing to do with Indian culture or Indian affairs."[39] In fact, to maintain a veneer of unity, the BBC wanted to avoid anything that might hint at Indian dissatisfaction over British rule. News and commentary were carefully screened and contained an English bias. Obviously, this wasn't the sort of job for Orwell. He held the job for two years and maintained that those years were simply wasted. However, the job did have the benefit of allowing Orwell to meet literary giants such as Dylan Thomas, T. S. Eliot, and J. B. Priestley. During these two years, Orwell did not write much and referred to his time at the BBC as a "mixture of whoreshop and lunatic asylum."[40]

Orwell resigned from the BBC in 1943 and began work for a left-wing journal called *Tribune*. The position was a much better fit for his skills and temperament. Orwell was literary editor and contributed a column to the magazine called "As I Please," which "tapped his eccentric interests"[41] ranging from a critique of Charles Dickens's *A Christmas Carol* to commenting on personal ads in a paper called the *Matrimonial Post and Fashionable Marriage Advertiser*. It is Orwell at his finest. In a piece dated July 14, 1944, Orwell writes he has received a number of letters protesting an earlier column in which he took aim at an anti-bombing pamphlet that was circulating at the time. In rebuttal, he addresses the misconception that Britain was "the first country to practise systematic bombing of civilians."[42] He points out that in the present war, it was the Germans who bombed Poland and Barcelona, the Italians who have bombed Abyssinia, and the Japanese who have bombed numerous Chinese cities.

I am not arguing that two blacks make a white, nor that Britain's record is a particularly good one . . . from about 1920 onwards the RAF has dropped its bombs on Afghans, Indians and Arabs who had little or no power of hitting back. But it is simply untruthful to say that large-scale bombing of crowded town areas with object of causing panic, is a British invention.[43]

He goes on to point out that "the parrot cry 'killing women and children,'" also needs some clarification: "It is probably somewhat better to kill a cross-section of the population than to kill only the young men,"[44] since in his mind if you accept killing at all, one life is not more valuable than another. Using his signature logic and irony, Orwell proceeds to his ultimate point:

> I have no enthusiasm for air raids, either our or the enemy's. Like a lot of other people in this country, I am growing definitely tired of bombs. But I do object to the hypocrisy of accepting force as an instrument while squealing against this or that individual weapon, or of denouncing war while wanting to preserve the kind of society that makes war inevitable.[45]

> **irony**
>
> The use of words to convey a meaning that is opposite of its usual meaning.

By the time he left *Tribune* in January 1945, Orwell had written more than one hundred essays, book reviews, and pieces for his column. Importantly, working at *Tribune* had given Orwell the time to complete *Animal Farm*, his first real masterpiece.

Though Orwell finished writing *Animal Farm* in February 1944, it took him over a year to find a publisher. Biographer John Rossi explains, "With its clever satire of the failures of the

THE REAL GEORGE ORWELL?

George Orwell was always ready to cast a critical eye on what he thought was unjust or unfair. Some point to his gifts of observation and high-minded principles that caused him to confront rather than to shy away from difficult issues, while others say Orwell was anti-Semitic, misogynistic, and a homophobe. "His central female characters, cannot be described as deep thinkers. Even the rebellious Julia in 1984 falls asleep during political discussion."[46] Biographer Michael Sheldon describes some of Orwell's relations, the proposals he made near the end of his life; while they may have been a bid for keeping his legacy alive, they also show a certain kind of discomfort or even desperation. His letters show "he was awkward in romantic matters and was slow to assert himself,"[47] while other biographers report that he was intentionally deceptive in his relations with women.[48] The picture one forms is of a contradictory and complicated man. Whatever he was, he was a man of his time. In evaluating his life and work, one must keep that in mind.

Russian Revolution and the brutalities of Stalin in the form of beast fable, *Animal Farm* was politically unacceptable in the midst of a war in which the Soviet Union and Great Britain were fighting as allies."[49] When the novel was finally published in August of 1945, World War II was over and Britain and the USSR were no longer allies. The book did phenomenally well, first in England and then in the United States where it became a Book-of-the-Month Club top seller. This success catapulted Orwell from an obscure political writer to a well-known author. Sales of the novel also made him financially secure. These achievements, however, were overshadowed by the fact that Orwell's wife had died in March 1945. The couple had an adopted son, Richard, whom Orwell would raise on his own.

Because of *Animal Farm*'s success, Orwell was able to move from London to Jura, an island off the coast of Scotland. In 1946, Orwell bought a large farmhouse called Barnhill. It had no electricity and the nearest neighbor was a mile away. But Orwell wanted to spend time writing without distraction—his own health was beginning to take its toll—and he thought he would be able to convince his friends to visit. The house was large enough to accommodate company and yet afford him privacy when he needed to work. It was on Jura that Orwell began his final masterpiece, *Nineteen Eighty-Four*.

In December 1947, Orwell suffered another attack of tuberculosis, which required that he spend seven months in a sanatorium. He was not allowed to write, but when released in July 1948, he went straight to Barnhill to complete *Nineteen Eighty-Four*. By January 1949, Orwell was again in hospital. In June, when the novel appeared, he was still there. Once again, the book was a success both in Britain and the United States. But George Orwell did not have long to enjoy its success. In September, he was moved to a hospital in London and in January 1950, he died. He was

fable

A brief tale with a moral or lesson.

satire

A way of using humor or sarcasm to ridicule human weakness or foolishness.

forty-six and at the height of his career. He is buried in All Saints Cemetery, Sutton Courtenay, Berkshire, England. On this tombstone are the simple words: "Here lies Eric Arthur Blair, born June 25th 1903, died January 21st 1950."

AUTOBIOGRAPHICAL JOURNALISM

Many critics argue that George Orwell was not a particularly gifted novelist, but as a "controversial critic and pamphleteer he was superb."[1] He had a keen eye, a precise writing style, and an unwavering sense of conviction. English professor James Seaton states, "Orwell's essays and journalism are permanently important not because of the political opinions they express but because, when taken as a whole, they articulate a distinctive point of view, a way of looking at the world, a perspective on life comparable in scope, depth, and intensity to that of a great novelist (which Orwell was not)."[2] In this chapter, we consider his autobiographical work and examine how, taken with his novels, we can gain a more complete understanding of Orwell as social commentator.

Down and Out in Paris and London

Published in 1933, Orwell's first full-length book exhibits his signature technique of combining journalism with autobiography. The work is an account of poverty in two cities. In Paris, the narrator, a version of Orwell, is close to poverty and finds work as a dishwasher in a large, exclusive hotel. The job pays barely enough for him to live on, and he works long hours in the dirty, hot kitchen. Orwell's descriptions, based on his own experiences, are detailed: the street on which he lives is "a ravine of tall, leprous houses, lurching toward one another in queer attitudes, as though they had all been frozen in the act of collapse,"[3] while his particular building is "a dark rickety warren of five storeys."[4] He draws a vivid picture of the people who inhabit this world: the Rougiers who sell pornographic postcards; Henri, who works in the sewers; R, the Englishman who lived in Putney with his parents six months of the year and in France for the other six, drinking himself silly. Then there is Boris, the White Russian; formerly of the Second Siberian Rifles Regiment of the Russian army, he works now as a waiter but dreams of owning his own hotel on the Right Bank.

In *Down and Out in Paris and London,* Orwell describes the squalor he witnessed in his travels: "The Paris slums are a gathering-place for eccentric people—people who have fallen into solitary, half-mad grooves of life and given up trying to be normal or decent."

However, the real focus is the dishwasher and his existence in the bowels of the hotel. Through this persona, Orwell communicates his views on poverty, "on its boredom, uselessness, hopelessness, squalor and brutalization."[5] The dishwasher himself "represents slavery in its many forms."[6] Orwell tells us that poverty is complicated: "it tangles you in a net of lies and even with the lies you can hardly manage it."[7] Lies and illusion are everywhere, like the pawn shop and the jail with the French motto—*Liberté*, Égalité, *Fraternité*—or "the trick of smacking one's cheeks to give the glow of health when looking for a job, or of rubbing garlic on bread to give the feeling of having eaten recently, the ruses to dodge the rent."[8] The lies and illusions all come together in Orwell's description of Hotel X, where only a door separates the hell of the kitchen from the elegant dining room. "However, even the dining room is a cheat, for it symbolizes not oppression but illusion. The gleam and elegance is all in the silverware and the linen. The food may have rolled in the sawdust or been spit upon by a raging waiter who serves it smilingly two minutes later. Corruption is everywhere."[9]

Orwell found that the same was true for London: "When you haven't a penny in your pocket you begin to see any city and any country in the most unfavorable light."[10]

Road to Wigan Pier

While *Down and Out in Paris and London* is usually cataloged as fiction, *The Road to Wigan Pier* is considered to be a work of social science and is cataloged as nonfiction. This is interesting, since Orwell employs many of the same techniques as in *Down and Out*.

In 1936, Orwell's publisher, Victor Gollancz, commissioned him to write about workers and economic conditions in northern England, a part of the country in which there were a large number of coal mines. As Bowker notes, these coal mines employed over a million workers at the time and relations between the miners and mine owners had always been tense. "Faced with lives destroyed by exploitation, he directed his sociological eye not just outwards on the grim landscape, but inwards, too, on his own inner turmoil. *The Road to Wigan Pier* would be both a factual account of a social enquiry and a personal record of conversion."[11]

A group of British coal miners emerge from the mine on a trolley in the 1930s. Orwell contemplated the lot of the working class in *The Road to Wigan Pier*: "If there is one man to whom I do feel myself inferior, it is a coal-miner."

Orwell traveled to Wigan, a small town in Greater Manchester, where he first stayed with an unemployed miner and International Labor Party worker. He then spent four nights at a boarding house "experiencing the unemployed working class at close quarters, noting living conditions and incomes of fellow lodgers."[12] He went to National Unemployed Workers Union meetings and eventually moved to a rooming house (the Brookers), which he describes as disgusting. "[A] once-gaudy carpet ringed by the slop-pails of years, and two gilt chairs with burst seats, and one of those old-fashioned horsehair armchairs which you slide off when you try to sit on them"[13] adorn the drawing room-turned-bedroom, which contains "four squalid beds."[14] The dining table is even worse, covered with newspapers and Worcester sauce and the crumbs of previous meals. Mr. Brooker prepared meals and sold tripe (animal stomach prepared for eating) in a shop at the front of the rooming house.

Orwell took a trip down a 900-foot (274-meter) mine shaft and recounts bending over for three-quarters of a mile (1.2 km). For someone who was six foot three (190 centimeters) and already had a weak chest, going into the mine was grueling. Yet his descriptions of the miners and other working people are not terribly complimentary. For example, he describes one of his landlord's son as a "large pig-like man,"[15] Mrs. Brooker is a "soft mound of fat and self-pity" who endlessly repeats herself, and a fellow boarder who is Scots is "a bore."[16] The social critic in him observes:

> [I]t is no use saying that people like the Brookers are just disgusting and trying to put them out of mind. For they exist in the tens and hundreds of thousands: they are one of the characteristic by-products of the modern world. You cannot disregard them if you accept the civilisation

that produced them. For this is part at least of what industrialism has done for us."[17]

Orwell acknowledges his bourgeois tendencies and confronts them directly. In chapter two, he points out the humiliation of watching coal miners at work: "It raises in you a momentary doubt about your own status as an 'intellectual' and a superior person generally. For it is brought home to you, at least while you are watching, that it is only because miners sweat their guts out that superior persons can remains superior."[18] Orwell expands this theme in the second part of the book particularly when he observes, "I shared bedrooms with miners, drank beer with them, played darts with them, talked to them by the hour together. But though I was among them, and I hope and trust they did not find me a nuisance, I was not one of them, and they knew it even better than I did."[19]

In the second part of the book, Orwell demonstrates his "gift for controversy"[20] by writing that "the worst arguments for socialism were the socialists themselves."[21] Orwell takes on socialist ideals and refutes them to the point that his editor wrote a forword in which he warns the reader that Orwell is "writing precisely as a member of the 'lower-upper-middle class' and when he describes Socialists as 'a stupid, offensive and insincere lot,' he is at one and the same time an extreme intellectual and a violent anti-intellectual . . . a frightful snob . . . and a genuine hater of every form of snobbery."[22]

Such, Such Were the Joys

Published posthumously in 1952 (in the United Kingdom, the collection was published as *England, Your England*), this collection contains an often quoted essay of the same name. Orwell borrowed the title from a poem by William Blake:

Such, such were the joys,
When we all girls & boys,
In our youth-time were seen
On the Echoing Green.

The essay chronicles Orwell's time at St. Cyprian's, which he refers to as "Crossgates," describing the horrors he endured as a scholarship boy. In contrast to the idyllic scene in Blake's verse, Orwell recalls the hard beds and horrible food, the door-less bathrooms and the general squalor of the school. But more than the physical discomforts, Orwell takes care to describe a "profound moral unease."[23] A few paragraphs into "Such, Such Were the Joys," Orwell's narrator tells us that he was caned for bedwetting and then because he told another boy that it hadn't hurt, he was beaten again. After being cross-examined by the headmistress who has overheard the comment, he is sent to the headmaster, who hits him so hard with a riding crop that the "bone handle went flying across the room"[24] while the headmaster reprimands the boy for breaking the crop. Furthermore, the boy feels actual shame, which, of course, is the point. Commentator Sam Leith writes,

Orwell zeroes in on the idea that here was a regime (the term seems apt) whose assumptions about the order of the universe are contradictory and unjust—yet at the same time unquestioningly internalised by its subjects. He hated Flip and Sambo (nicknames for the real head-mistress and headmaster of St. Cyprian's) and yet knew them to be his benefactors. He had no control over his bedwetting—though he prayed fervently for it to stop—yet was conscious of it as sin.[25]

Leith finds this essay to be a "very odd piece of writing," observing that given Orwell's propensity for analyzing culture, this work is

> absolutely sodden with self-pity. [W]hile you might expect it to show Orwell in analytical mode—a meditation on the way in which the private school system internalises expectations to do with class and hierarchy— you find none of that detachment. It hints at those themes but it is agonizingly personal, a howl of grievance when it is not a yelp of derisive laughter.[26]

Orwell himself says in the essay: "Whoever writes about his childhood must beware of exaggeration and self-pity."[27]

Another Orwell critic, D. J. Taylor, contends that the piece was conceived when "Orwell was incubating or writing, what became *Nineteen Eighty-Four*."[28] For Taylor, this connection to that famous novel makes the piece all the more fascinating.

> If you go back and read the descriptions of O'Brien, he is described as being first like a priest and then like a schoolmaster. It's almost like Winston Smith is the boy he is trying to reform. And I'm interested by all the totalitarian language in "Such, Such." Which piece came first—you can argue either way. In some ways the chronology isn't even important.[29]

Taylor asserts that many critics have speculated that this essay, essentially an exposé of totalitarianism, is proof that Orwell was destined to become a socialist from an early age. "But it could be argued, equally plausibly, that the trick is being played the other way round—that Orwell's mature views on authoritarianism and its psychological consequences encouraged him to recast his memories of St. Cyprian's in a more sinister shape.[30] Taylor also admonishes us to consider the isolation of the writer in "Such, Such Were the Joys." "This is what Orwell does with his novels: he creates this almost entirely alone and friendless character at the mercy of vast and unappeasable forces that he or she has no way of comprehending or dealing with—and then the walls close in . . . And exactly the same trick is played here."[31]

The essay was deemed too libelous to print when Orwell wrote it, and it didn't appear in print in England until 1968 when headmistress Mrs. Wilkes was long dead. But it is a prime example of the sort of journalistic autobiography Orwell excelled at writing. By discussing English mores and camouflaging the identity of the school that cause him "memories of disgust," he blurs the line between truth and fiction.

ANIMAL TALE

Despite the slimness of the novel, *Animal Farm* changed Orwell's career, making him a best-selling author not only in England but in America and other countries as well. Given the difficulty he experienced getting the book published, Orwell certainly could not have foreseen the novel's enormous success.

According to biographer Michael Sheldon, the idea for *Animal Farm* was cemented while Orwell was fighting in Spain. "Having barely escaped from the long reach of Stalin's agents, he began to reflect on how a genuine revolutionary movement in Spain could have allowed itself to come so completely under the control of a dictator living thousands of miles away."[1] What Orwell wanted to convey to readers was the myth of Soviet-style socialism, and he wanted to do this in a creative way. Sheldon explains, "What better way to fight that myth than to create a mythical story of animals whose successful revolt against tyranny degenerates into a greedy struggle for power?"[2] On a superficial level, the story is so simple that even a child can understand it.

However, the key to really understanding this novel lies in knowing something about its historical context. As Orwell expert John Rodden says, "We need to understand how in the first half of the century Communism and anti-Communism were among the most significant issues in American and British political affairs. And to do this, we need to understand

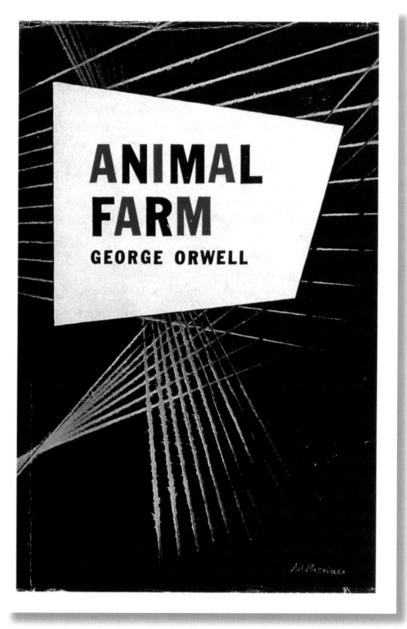

The original full title, *Animal Farm: A Fairy Story*, was changed when some publishers dropped the subtitle because it gave the impression of a children's book.

the original political background of that period, against which Orwell wrote his book."[3] Orwell himself believed that a writer's subject matter "will be determined by the age he lives in."[4] Even with a simplified understanding of what caused the rise and fall of the Soviet Union, says Rodden, readers will find that "*Animal Farm* captures both the hope and the tragedy of the Russian Revolution and that it provides an introduction to a few of the major figures in the history of Communism."[5]

As Orwell was working on *Animal Farm*, World War II raged, and the United States, Britain, and the Soviet Union had joined into a tenuous alliance. Michael Sheldon, among others, notes: "Many influential people in Britain did not want to risk giving serious offense to the Soviet dictator at this crucial period in the war."[6] Publishers in Britain were particularly sensitive to anything that could be construed as anti-Soviet and claimed that to criticize would be to play into the hands of the Nazis. Orwell rejected this idea as "a charm or incantation used to silence uncomfortable truths."[7]

Four publishers rejected the manuscript, including Gollancz, the publisher with whom Orwell had a contract. Finally, Fredric Warburg accepted the manuscript but had to delay its publication due to wartime paper rationing. By the time the book appeared, Hitler had been defeated and Stalin was no longer an ally.

Cast of Characters

Orwell scholar John Rossi says Orwell drew many of the names for the novel from his past. When he lived in Wallington, England, he had a neighbor called Mr. Jones, and there was a farm called Manor Farm near where Orwell lived as a boy in Sussex.[8] The following is a list of the characters who

RUSSIAN REVOLUTION AND THE RISE OF COMMUNISM

The Russian Revolution of 1917 actually took place in two phases. The first phase, in February, achieved the overthrow of Czar Nicholas II. The second phase, in October, succeeded in installing the Bolsheviks as leaders, one of whom was Vladimir Ilich Lenin.

The people of Russia had grown tired of the czar's corrupt government and his reactionary policies—he occasionally would dissolve the Russian parliament (or Duma)—and they were hungry. After Russia's catastrophic losses in World War I, there were food shortages, land grabs, and nationalist movements that threatened to topple the already unstable government. The Bolsheviks, with Lenin as their leader, campaigned on a platform of "peace, land, and bread," which appealed to the hungry urban workers and soldiers. Along with the Left Socialist Revolutionary Party, the Bolsheviks were able to stage a bloodless coup, seizing government buildings, telegraph stations, and other strategic facilities.

After October, the Bolsheviks would not share power with any revolutionary group except the Left Socialist Revolutionary Party, suppressing any opposition. They became the Russian Communist Party (of Bolsheviks) in March 1918; the All-Union Communist Party (of Bolsheviks) in December 1925; and finally the Communist Party of the Soviet Union (CCCP) in 1952. These name changes also reflected the ideological fighting within the party, to which Orwell alludes in *Animal Farm* and *Nineteen Eighty-Four*.

It was into the All-Union Communist Party that Joseph Stalin was admitted, along with Leon Trotsky, who would become Stalin's chief rival. When Lenin died in January 1924, Stalin took over the party leadership and abandoned many of Lenin's economic policies. When Stalin's ally Nikolay Bukharin protested Stalin's policies of rapid industrialization and collectivization, Stalin got rid of him. To eliminate any more opposition, Stalin launched the Great Purge (1934–1938), in which many thousands of his real or assumed opponents were executed as traitors and millions more were imprisoned or sent to forced-labor camps in remote places like Siberia. During Stalin's rule, the party expanded from approximately 470,000 members in 1924 to several million from the 1930s onward. Orwell would have known much about how Stalin came to power and turned the ideal of communism into totalitarianism.

Revolutionaries storm the Winter Palace during the Russian Revolution in 1917. The event marked the overthrow of the monarchy by the Bolsheviks, an insurrection that is satirized in the animals' takeover of Manor Farm.

inhabit *Animal Farm*, along with some suggestions about their significance to the plot.

Napoleon is the embodiment of Stalin. Described as "large, rather fierce-looking Berkshire boar, the only Berkshire on the farm, not much of a talker, but with a reputation for getting his own way,"[9] he appears to be more interested in power than ideology. He, along with the other pigs Snowball and Squealer, can read and write. They are the ones who author the Seven Commandments and write them on the barn wall for all to see. "The key role played by the pigs parallels the Communist Party elite."[10] Shortly after the animals' successful takeover of Manor Farm, Napoleon takes nine puppies to educate them, claiming that the most important thing for the future is the education (e.g., indoctrinate) of young minds. In the end, these dogs grow up to be Napoleon's bodyguards and secret police. The similarities to Joseph Stalin are uncanny. Just as Stalin negotiated with Britain while secretly dealing with Hitler, so, too, Napoleon negotiates with "either Mr. Pilkington of Foxwood or with Mr. Frederick of Pinchfield—but never, it was noticed, with both simultaneously."[11]

Napoleon's relationship with Snowball reflects that of Stalin with Leon Trotsky. As one of the architects of the Soviet Union, it was assumed Trotsky would take over from Lenin, who died in 1924. Stalin, however, wanted the power and had a reputation for eliminating anyone who stood in his way. He had Trotsky barred from office (Trotsky had made plenty of enemies as a revolutionary before the Soviet Union came into existence) and then was able to expel him from the country. Once Trotsky was in exile, Stalin ordered him assassinated. In 1940, in Mexico City, Trotsky was fatally wounded with an ice pick at the hands of Russian assassin Ramon Mercador. In the same way, Napoleon runs Snowball off the farm, kills the animals who confess to being Snowball's allies, and makes Snowball responsible for all that goes wrong on the farm.

At the end of the novel, we see Napoleon walking on two legs, just like the humans he had previously condemned. He says that Animal Farm will again be called Manor Farm and gives the same toast he gave at the beginning of the book, "but in a different form," underscoring a theme Orwell will again take up in *Nineteen Eighty-Four*—the corrupting influence of power.[12]

Snowball is the "vivacious," "inventive" pig who speaks animatedly but is "not considered to have the same depth of character" as Napoleon.[13] It is he who translates Old Major's vision into the seven principles of Animalism, organizes animals into various committees (the Egg Production Committee for the hens, the Clean Tails League for the cows, and the Whiter Wool Movement for the sheep), and strategizes the farm's defense against the humans. In the Battle of the Cowshed, Snowball is praised for his military prowess, for which he wins a medal. And it is Snowball who wants to build a windmill so the farm can produce electricity. Snowball is Leon Trotsky. When Napoleon runs Snowball off the farm, it parallels Stalin's exiling Trotsky from Russia. With Snowball out of the way, Napoleon blames him for everything that goes wrong, the same way that Stalin blamed his former partner Trotsky. And just as in Russia in the 1930s when Trotsky's former acolytes were forced to confess to crimes they may or may not have committed, the animals must confess to conspiring with Snowball to topple the remaining pigs. In real life and on Animal Farm, conspirators are killed.

Old Major is a prize Middle White boar. Though old, he is still a "majestic-looking pig, with a wise and benevolent appearance in spite of the fact that his tushes had never been cut."[14] If you look at a picture Karl Marx you will see the description is apt: For much of his adult life Marx wore a distinctively bushy mustache and beard. Clearly, Old Major is Orwell's stand-in for Karl Marx. It is he who initially gathers the animals and relates to them his dream, a vision of the world in which animals (or in Marxist terms, the working man) would rule the world. He is the one who teaches the animals the original rallying cry of the animal rebellion, "Beasts of England." In short, like Marx, Old Major is the one with the original ideas, the pure philosophy.

Boxer is one of the two cart horses on the farm, "an enormous beast, nearly eighteen hands high, and as strong as any two ordinary horses put together." He is strong but sensitive, and when he accidentally kills a stable hand during the Battle of the Cowshed, he is full of remorse, saying, "I have no wish to take life, not even a human life."[15]

Benjamin the donkey is devoted to Boxer, who in turn believes everything that Napoleon and Snowball tell him. He repeats their slogans and works slavishly to complete their projects. When it becomes clear that he can no longer work, Napoleon has Boxer sent to a horse processing plant.

Russian dictator Joseph Stalin is represented by Napoleon, the main villain of *Animal Farm*.

Symbolically, Boxer represents the working-class people who accept their circumstances because they believe that hard work will help them to get ahead and that their leaders will protect them.

Squealer is the small, fat pig who has "very round cheeks, twinkling eyes, nimble movements, and a shrill voice." A "brilliant talker," he can argue any point and "has a way of skipping from side to side and whisking his tail" that is extremely persuasive. The other animals say that Squealer can turn "black to white." Squealer has an explanation for everything: why the pigs need to confiscate the milk and apples, why the Seven Commandments seem to change, why the "veterinarian" who comes to take Boxer has a truck with the words "Horse Slaughterer" on it. In the end, Squealer is so fat that he could only with "difficulty see out of his eyes," and when he walks appears walking on two legs "[a] little awkwardly, as though not quite used to supporting his considerable bulk," he has already prepared the sheep to recite a new slogan "Four legs, two legs *better*!"[16]

In Orwell's allegory, Squealer represents all the ways that the Communist Party spread propaganda, in particular the former Soviet Union's official newspaper *Pravda*. (Interestingly, this word means "truth" in Russian. The word "squeal" can mean to tell someone in authority about a wrong-doing, but it can also mean to tattle on or betray others.)

Mr. Jones and Mr. Frederick are farm owners. Jones, the original owner of Manor Farm, unwittingly inspires the animals to rebel when he gets drunk and fails to do his chores around the farm. He attempts to get his farm back but cannot and eventually ends up dying in "an inebriates' home."[17] By giving this farmer such a common name as "Jones," Orwell seems to be saying that the farmer could be any man. But reading the work as a political satire, Jones can be likened to Czar Nicholas II, who was easily toppled in the Russian Revolution of 1917.

Frederick, on the other hand, represents Hitler, and his farm is Nazi Germany. The timber agreement that Napoleon brokers with him is symbolic of the Nazi-Soviet Nonaggression Pact of August 1939 in which Germany and Russia agreed they would not attack each other independently or with the help of other powers. The pact redrew borders of countries such as Poland, Lithuania, Latvia, Estonia, and Finland to spheres of Soviet or German influence. Through this agreement, Hitler was able to attack Poland and begin World War II. Stalin had faithfully lived up to the pact with the Germans for two years, even sending supplies to Germany on the very day Germany attacked the Soviet Union. Critic David Dawn writes, "Napoleon's anger when he discovers the forged bank notes parallels Stalin's sense of betrayal after the German attack on the Soviet Union in June 1941. We know that Stalin at first refused to believe the news of Hitler's treachery."[18] Then he fought back, just as the animals do. However, the loss of life on Animal Farm is great, just as the Soviet people suffered during the war.

Benjamin, a donkey, is the oldest animal on the farm as well as "the worst tempered." He is also the most cynical on the farm, believing that no matter what the animals do, "life will go on as it always gone on—that is, badly." Though he can "read as well as any pig," he usually refuses to. In Benjamin, Orwell has created an intellectual cynic, the type of person who does not believe in political change and therefore does not get involved.[19]

allegory

A story in which characters and events are symbolic of real life and events.

Clover is the other cart horse. Orwell describes her as "a stout motherly mare approaching middle life."[20] Like Boxer, she believes in Napoleon; for example, she confronts Mollie for talking to a human. Unlike Boxer, however, Clover questions some of the changes the pigs make to the doctrine of Animalism. Even so, she accepts Squealer's explanation of the changes and can do nothing when Boxer is taken away. In her, Orwell has created a character who represents those in the working class who recognize on some level that they are being exploited but because of their own limitations or apathy do nothing.

Mr. Pilkington owns Foxwood, one of the farms neighboring Jones's. Orwell describes Foxwood as "a large, neglected, old-fashioned farm, much overgrown by woodland, with all its pastures worn out and its hedges in a disgraceful condition."[21] Pilkington is an "easy-going gentleman farmer who spent most of his time fishing and hunting."

Mollie, the "foolish, pretty white mare," used

Philosopher Karl Marx's beliefs about economics and class struggles helped to lay the groundwork for the Russian communist movement. In a similar way, Old Major plants the seeds for revolution at the start of *Animal Farm*.

to drive Mr. Jones's carriage. Her concerns are for her own comfort. When Old Major talks about rebellion, she wants to make sure she has enough sugar and ribbons. Eventually, she goes to work for a human, apparently enjoying herself and "[n]one of the animals ever mentioned Mollie again." Mollie represents those who are dazzled by material possessions, rather than ideals and who fail to see the importance of having freedom.[22]

Minimus is a poet of the rebellion. Orwell does not describe him as much more, but we learn that he wrote a poem to honor Napoleon and is also responsible for rewriting the lyrics to "Beasts of England." He embodies poets like Vlad-

Czar Nicholas II, seen here with his family, was forced to abdicate the throne after the February Revolution of 1917 and was killed, along with his family, the following year. The ousting of Mr. Jones in *Animal Farm* is meant to represent the czar's overthrow.

imir Mayakovsky who allowed the Soviet state to use them for political purposes.

Moses is a tame raven who was "Jones's especial pet" and is considered a spy and tale-bearer but also a "clever talker."[23] He appears after the rebellion and is symbolic of the Russian Orthodox Church, which was state-controlled after the revolution. When Moses speaks of the wonderful Sugarcandy Mountain, Orwell is rather comically referring to Marx's famous line about religion being the opiate of the masses. When the animals decide to turn the farmhouse into a museum, Orwell is suggesting that this is exactly what the Communists did to the Russian Orthodox Church.

Muriel is named after an actual goat Orwell owned. She reads better than some of the dogs, and when Clover wants to check the Seven Commandments to see whether they have been altered, it is Muriel who helps her read the revision.

Mr. Wymper is the attorney that Napoleon chooses to handle pig-human negotiations. He is always happy to do what is advantageous to him and not particularly concerned about ethics. He represents the go-between who intervenes on behalf of warring countries, not particularly concerned about what is right and wrong, but interested in expediency.

The Sheep are never mentioned as individuals and always act as a group. They are too stupid to learn all the Seven Commandments by heart but do bleat slogans endlessly. In this way, they represent those in society who can repeat the party line but never really examine what they are saying.

Plot

In the book's opening scene we meet Mr. Jones, owner of the Manor Farm. Presumably he's a drinker because as he secures the farm for the night, he lurches across the yard and before turning in, draws himself a last glass of beer from the keg in the kitchen. Once he is off in bed, Old Major, the twelve-year-old prize pig calls a meeting. He is "so highly regarded on the farm that everyone was quite ready to lose an hour's sleep in order to hear what he had to say."[24]

In this chapter we are introduced to most of the animal cast: the dogs Bluebell, Jessie, and Pincer; the cart horses Boxer and Clover; Muriel the goat; and Benjamin the donkey. Major says that he has been thinking about the treatment of English animals. "We are born, we are given just so much food as will keep the breath in our bodies and those of us who are capable of it are forced to work to the last atom of our strength." The farm can supply all the animals' needs, Major tells them, but humans have been reaping the benefit of all the animals' labors. In this observation, Orwell equates Manor Farm to his vision of Russia: a potentially prosperous country that has been poorly governed. Major believes that the animals must rebel against their human oppressors and live peacefully with all other animals. "And, above all, no animal must tyrannise his own kind," he states. The chapter ends with Major teaching the animals "Beasts of England," "a stirring tune," that will become the anthem of the animals, just as "The Internationale" has been the signature song of socialists since the nineteenth century.[25]

Soon after giving his speech, Old Major dies. The pigs Snowball, Napoleon, and Squealer expand on Major's ideas to create Animalism, a philosophy that preaches equality among animals. The opportunity for rebellion comes more much more quickly than expected. Mr. Jones leaves the farm on Saturday night to visit a pub and doesn't come back until midday Sunday. As the animals have not been fed, one of the cows breaks into the food shed and all the animals begin helping themselves. When Mr. Jones and the farmhands attempt to stop them, the animals succeed in running the humans off the farm, destroying anything that reminds them of their former oppressors.

The pigs soon reveal that during the past three months, they have taught themselves to read and write. Snowball gets a paintbrush and a bucket of paint and renames the farm "Animal Farm." The pigs also explain that by their studies of the past months, they have "succeeded in reducing the principles of Animalism to Seven Commandments." These are now inscribed on the wall of the big barn, and they "form an unalterable law by which all of the animals on Animal Farm must live for ever after."[26]

The laws are as follows:

1. Whatever goes upon two legs is an enemy.
2. Whatever goes upon four legs, or has wings, is a friend.
3. No animal shall wear clothes.
4. No animal shall sleep in a bed.
5. No animal shall drink alcohol.
6. No animal shall kill another animal.
7. All animals are equal.

The animals make a plan to harvest the hayfield, but before they can begin work several of the cows must be milked. The pigs take care of this chore, and when the question of what to do with the milk comes up, it is put off for a later time as they must get to the fields. The milk is gone when they return.

The farm enjoys a time of harmony in which all the animals work together and make the harvest successful. Every week there is a meeting to discuss plans for the farm's future. Because many of the animals are unable to read or remember the Seven Commandments, Snowball simplifies these directives: "Four legs good, two legs bad." Napoleon, feeling that "the education of the young was more important than anything that could be done for those who were already grown up," takes any newborn animals away from their mothers and "kept them in such seclusion that the rest of the farm soon forgot their existence."[27]

The animals soon learn that all of the milk and apples on the farm will be given to the pigs. Some of them object, but to no avail. Squealer is called upon to explain this latest development to his "comrades." He says that they are mistaken if they believe the pigs are selfish. In fact, he says that many pigs do not like these foods but that because they are the "brains" behind Animal Farm, they must keep up their health, and milk and apples are essential for that; it is a scientific fact. "We pigs are the brainworkers . . . Day and night we are watching over your welfare. It is for *your* sake that we drink the milk and eat those apples."[28] This passage is an example of foreshadowing: It would appear that some animals are more equal than others. (In fact, later in the novel

Bolshevik leader Leon Trotsky was ultimately exiled in much the same way that Snowball is run off by Napoleon.

the Seventh Commandment of Animalism is adapted to this effect.) But Orwell is also using the animals to illustrate class conflict. Having witnessed unequal treatment in boarding school and then watched the British ruling class in Burma, Orwell concludes that the classless society is far from attainable. The diversion of milk and apples to the pigs is just the beginning of the privileges they will enjoy.

As the news of Animal Farm spreads across the English countryside, more and more animals are learning "Beasts of England." For his part, Jones has been sitting in the pub "complaining to anyone who would listen of the monstrous injustice he had suffered" by being thrown off his own property by a "pack of good-for-nothing animals." The owners of two neighboring farms, Pilkington and Frederick, laugh at Jones at first. But as the days march on and it appears the animals are running Jones's farm, the two decide they will reclaim Animal Farm. With Snowball in the lead, crying "War is War," and "the only good human being is a dead one," the animals fight off the humans in the Battle of the Cowshed. After this confrontation, all of the animals decide to bestow the newly created military honor, "Animal Hero, First Class," upon Snowball.[29]

Napoleon and Snowball begin to clash over numerous issues. "If one of them suggested sowing a bigger acreage with barley, the other was certain to demand a bigger acreage of oats, and if one of them said that such and such a field was just right for cabbages, the other would declare that it was useless for anything accept roots."[30] Then there is the subject of the windmill. Snowball has designed it and contends that while it will be hard to build, it will save so much time that the animals will only need to work for three days each week. Napoleon argues that food production is the farm's most important immediate goal and that efforts should be focused on that.

As the debate reaches fever pitch, "nine enormous dogs wearing brass-studded collars" come into the barn and charge Snowball. Snowball is chased from the farm, and Napoleon takes over. His first step is to announce that the planning meetings are over. Then Squealer tries to convince everyone that Snowball is a criminal. Three days after Snowball's expulsion, the animals are "somewhat surprised to hear Napoleon announce that the windmill will be built after all." Squealer convinces them that the idea was actually Napoleon's from the beginning, saying that Napoleon "*seemed* to oppose the windmill, simply as a manoeuvre to get rid of Snowball, who was a dangerous character and a bad influence."[31]

The following year, the animals work like slaves. Through the spring and summer, the workload is increased to sixty hours a week, and in August Napoleon announces that Sunday afternoons will be devoted to work as well. Though the work is "strictly voluntary," any animal who doesn't participate will have his or her rations halved. Then Napoleon announces he has decided that Animal Farm will now engage in trading with neighboring farms, not for "commercial purposes," but to get the materials needed for the windmill. The animals feel "a vague uneasiness" as Napoleon's announcement seems to violate several basic principles of Animalism: never deal with humans, never engage in trade, and never make use of money. But Squealer convinces them that "the resolution against engaging in trade and using money had never been passed, or even suggested." And to those animals expressing lingering doubts, Squealer asks, "Are you certain that this is not something that you dreamed comrades? Have you any record of such a resolution?" Meanwhile, the pigs have moved into the farmhouse and rumor has it they are sleeping in beds. The critical point, they argue, is that they are not sleeping in beds with *sheets*. Instead, they contend, the reason behind the Fourth Commandment was that sheets are a human invention. Curiously, the animals do not remember the part about the sheets, but when they consult the wall of the big barn, they see it says "No animal shall sleep in a bed *with sheets*."[32]

In the raging winds of November, progress on the windmill stops because it is too windy and wet to continue. "Finally there came a night when the gale was so violent that the farm buildings rocked on their foundations."[33] The severe weather also leaves the windmill in ruins. Napoleon claims that Snowball is responsible for the destruction, pronouncing a death sentence upon him and a reward for his capture. The animals begin the tedious process of rebuilding the windmill.

The bitter winter hinders the animals, but they continue building the windmill. Food shortages are common, and it becomes clear that Animal Farm must get grain from somewhere. The hens are informed that they must surrender their eggs because Napoleon has brokered a deal with a human called Whymper to exchange their eggs for the grain. When they protest, Napoleon withholds their rations and punishes any animal who is caught giving them food. Rumors circulate that Snowball is sneaking into the farm at night and stealing, trampling seedbeds, and overturning milk pails. In fact, whenever "anything went wrong it became usual to attribute it to Snowball." When the key of the storeroom shed can't be found, "the whole farm is convinced that Snowball had thrown it down the well. Curiously enough, they went on believing this even after the mislaid key was found under a sack of meal."[34]

Napoleon announces a full investigation of Snowball and demands that any animals who have had contact with him must confess. Those who do are ripped apart by Napoleon's dogs. The remaining animals are shaken. "In the old days there had often been scenes of bloodshed equally terrible, but it seemed to all of them that it was far worse now that it was happening among themselves."[35] And though Orwell does not repeat it in this chapter, we recall Commandment Six (No animal shall kill another animal) has been broken. While the remaining animals try to console themselves by singing "Beasts of England," Squealer and two dogs inform them that Comrade Napoleon has banned the song.

A few days after the slaughter, the animals finally remember the Sixth Commandment, but when they check the barn wall, it now reads: "No animal shall kill any other animal *without cause*." Napoleon continues to arrange deals with the humans, and the animals continue to work harder. Orders are issued through Squealer or another pig, and Napoleon is seen less often. When he does appear, he is called "our Leader, Comrade Napoleon" and a poem is written in his honor and inscribed on the barn wall.[36]

Through Mr. Whymper, Napoleon has negotiated to sell lumber to Mr. Pilkington, the human running Foxwood Farm, one of the properties that abuts Animal Farm. Though the animals mistrust him, they dislike Fredrick, the owner of Pinchfield (Animal Farm's other neighbor), even more. Terrible stories about Fredrick's treatment of his animals have been circulating, and even Napoleon says he is the enemy. The animals consider coming to aid those unfortunate enough to live at Pinchfield, but Squealer counsels caution. Then several days later Napoleon sells the timber to Fredrick and declares Pilkington the enemy.

It turns out that Fredrick has paid for the timber with forged money. Along with some other men, he attacks Animal

Farm and destroys their windmill. Squealer, always in the service of Napoleon (and "unaccountably absent during the fighting"), tells the animals that they have not been defeated but have won a victory by driving "the enemy off our soil—the sacred soil of Animal Farm." The animals discover a case of whisky in the farmhouse cellar, and that very night they hear loud celebration coming from the farmhouse. The very next morning, the animals are told that Napoleon is dying. A bit later in the day, Squealer announces that as one of his last decrees, Napoleon has determined that drinking alcohol is an act that is punishable by death. As evening approaches, Napoleon is reported to be in better condition, and by the evening of the next day, he is working. Rumor spreads that he has instructed Whymper to buy books on distilling and brewing. One week later, Napoleon has determined that the small paddock originally intended for grazing for animals who can longer work, will be dug up and sown with barley (a prime ingredient in beer and whisky). Not long afterward, the animals notice that the Fifth Commandment has been changed to "No animal shall drink alcohol *to excess.*"[37]

Another bitter winter sets in. Food rations have been reduced again for everyone but the pigs and the dogs. Boxer, the old cart horse, is ailing. Napoleon claims that Boxer is being taken to the hospital when in fact he is being taken to a slaughterhouse. Three days later when Boxer's death is announced, the animals question this rendition of truth—the truck that had collected Boxer had the words "Alfred Simmonds, Horse Slaughterer and Glue Boiler" inscribed on it. Again, Squealer equivocates, saying that, in fact, the truck belonged to a veterinarian who had not yet repainted the truck.

The years pass. Animals die and only a handful remember the original rebellion. The farm, though larger and prosperous, has not made the animals themselves any richer, "except, of course, for the pigs and the dogs."[38] Squealer continues spinning propaganda, claiming that the pigs' work in supervising and organizing the farm requires superior intelligence and "enormous labors" that the average animal could simply not understand.

One day a pig appears walking on hind legs. It is Squealer. Then a long line of pigs come out from the farmhouse, also on hind legs. Finally, Napoleon himself emerges, walking on two legs and "casting haughty glances from side to side."[39] The animals are stunned. But before they can say a word, the pigs begin to chant, "Four legs good, two legs better!" The Seven Commandments have disappeared from the barn wall, replaced by the statement: ALL ANIMALS ARE EQUAL BUT SOME ANIMALS ARE MORE EQUAL THAN OTHERS.

After this, it does not seem strange when the pigs begin carrying around whips, buy themselves a radio and telephone service, and subscribe to several newspapers. Napoleon begins wearing Mr. Jones's clothes, and Pilkington and Foxwood are now friends of the pigs. Finally, Napoleon announces that the name Animal Farm has been abolished, and that the correct and original name Manor Farm will be used henceforth. As the other animals peer through the window, they realize that they can no longer tell man and pig apart.

Themes

Politics and the English Language

Throughout his writing career, Orwell was very concerned with the way words were used. He wrote many pieces about the way he felt it was being used or abused. In an essay entitled "Politics and the English Language," he wrote that language

Russian peasants work in the fields shortly after the Russian Revolution. The life that they were promised did not come to fruition for many, and they were forced to toil for long hours.

"becomes ugly and inaccurate because our thoughts are foolish, but the slovenliness of our language makes it easier for us to have foolish thoughts."[40]

In *Animal Farm*, Orwell shows how those in power can manipulate words for their own purposes. For example, when the birds object to the slogan "Four legs good, two legs bad," Squealer launches into an explanation claiming that a wing is "an organ of propulsion and not of manipulation" so it is basically a leg. Here he demonstrates his gift for turning "black into white," much like Joseph Goebbels, the minister of propaganda for the Nazis, or the official news agency of Russia, TASS. So when the harsh winter means reduced food, Squealer calls it a "readjustment."[41]

In a talk called "Literature and Totalitarianism," Orwell warns that the age of the "autonomous individual" (or at least the illusion of autonomy) is at risk and that

> Totalitarianism has abolished freedom of thought to an extent unheard of in any previous age. And it is important to realize that its control of thought is not only negative, but positive. It not only forbids you to express—even to think—certain thoughts, but it dictates what you *shall* think, it creates an ideology for you, it tries to govern your emotional life as well as setting up a code of conduct. And as far as possible it isolates you from the outside world, it shuts you up in an artificial universe in which you have no standards of comparison. The totalitarian state tries, at any rate, to control the thoughts and emotions of its subjects at least as completely as it controls their actions.[42]

In *Animal Farm*, Squealer does precisely this when he tells the animals that Snowball had never received the medal of "Animal Hero, First Class," even though the animals themselves had created the award; that it was simply a rumor. In fact, "far from being decorated, he had been censured for showing cowardice in the battle."[43]

Religion

Orwell tended to view religion through a political lens. In particular, he saw Catholicism as "intellectually fashionable, hierarchically structured, and conservative or even fascist in political influence"[44] In *Animal Farm*, Moses the raven (who represents the church) gets special treatment, including not having to work and receiving a daily beer ration. Here Orwell is equating the bird's treatment with the way many totalitarian regimes treat the clergy as a privileged class, valued for their ability to mollify and subdue believers with the promise of rewards in the afterlife. Like Marx, Orwell saw religion as "another corruptible institution which serves to keep the masses tranquil."[45]

Class Conflict and Equality

Orwell acknowledged that everything he wrote was directly or indirectly related to his politics: "I write [it] because there is some lie I want to expose, some fact to which I want to draw attention."[46] Orwell had seen social hierarchies from the time he went to St. Cyprian's as a scholarship boy, in Burma as part of the British ruling class, and in Spain (and by extension Russia) as part of the Workers' Party of Marxist Unification. When *Animal Farm* begins, the animals are looking to reap the benefits of their labor, to eliminate men who keep them from wealth and freedom, and to make all animals equal. For some time the animals are "happy as they had never conceived it possible to be."[47] All are well fed, finding pleasure in food they have produced, and everyone works according to "his capacity."

The idyllic scene does not last. The pigs soon grab privileges, beginning with stealing the milk and apples. Soon the animals must step aside when they encounter a pig on the same path, and the pigs are allowed to wear (previously forbidden) green ribbons on Sundays. By this point, the other animals barely question these entitlements because the social order has already been established. In one scene, Pilkington says to Napoleon: "you have your lower animals to contend with, we have our lower classes" and then proceeds to fight over a playing card, and the animals "looked from pig to man and from man to pig and from pig to man again; but already it was impossible to say which was which," we know what Orwell is really saying is that a classless society, though a wonderful ideal, may not be achieved; in the end one dogma is indistinguishable from another.[48]

Style

Orwell uses a third-person, omniscient narrator to tell the story. Events are related without comment, leaving readers to draw their own conclusions about the injustices and unfairness the animals endure. The narrator's words (Mollie is "the foolish, pretty white mare," Major is "still a majestic-looking pig, with a wise and benevolent appearance") help to humanize the animals and makes us sympathetic readers. At the same time, the objective narration serves to emphasize the animals' lack of true understanding of their plight.

Fables and Fairy Tales

Fairy tales are a literary form found throughout the world. Most fairy tales include kings and queens, talking animals, rich and poor, good and bad. In fact, the world of fairy tales is one where good and evil are clear. Though they do not have an explicit moral the way fables do, fairy tales present moral choices between right and wrong. Orwell originally gave his work the title *Animal Farm: A Fairy Story*. By calling the novel a "fairy story," Orwell gives us the idea that the story's theme is universal, accessible to a reader from any culture. It is also an illustration of Orwell's sense of irony, since the story "behind" the story is far from simple.

Another common literary form found in almost every culture is the fable. Fables almost always have talking animals who take on human emotions like jealousy or greed. These stories have an explicit moral: two wrongs do not equal a right, a kindness is never wasted, it is easy to be brave when not in danger, and so on. Orwell gives his animals realistic details—Mollie likes her nose petted, the cat disappears for hours, and Benjamin the donkey is slow but steady—so that their human traits seem equally believable: the pigs are greedy power grabbers, the sheep are stupid and easily led, and the horses are sturdy, uncomplaining workers.

Women hand out issues of the Russian newspaper *Pravda* in the 1940s. The official paper of the communist party, *Pravda* contained propaganda that encouraged people to support the war. The pigs on *Animal Farm* distribute their own propaganda through slogans that change to suit their needs.

Other Literary Devices

An allegory is an extended metaphor: a story with meaning beyond the literal story. The writer's principle tool is personification; that is, giving abstract qualities human form (or animals human characteristics). This literary form was frequently used in Christian literature of the Middle Ages in which authors like William Langland (*Piers Plowman*) used allegory to represent the power of the church.

Orwell uses allegory in *Animal Farm* to create a satire—that is, a work that uses humor to criticize or show the weaknesses in a person, government, or society. He takes events from the Russian Revolution and brings them to the animal realm, so that they seem absurd. In so doing, he implies that real revolution and its promises of glory for the working man are also ridiculous.

Another literary device Orwell makes great use of is irony. In literature, irony is a way of creating meaning that is different from what one would expect, to say one thing and actually mean another (usually opposite) thing; for example, the phrase "clear as mud."

Irony is a way to call attention to absurdity, to create comedy or deepen a tragedy. With dramatic irony, which is what Orwell uses in *Animal Farm*, tension is created from what we know and what the animals and our naive narrator do not. When the horse slaughterer takes Boxer away, we already know why, but the animals do not. Squealer spins a yarn about the slaughterer actually being a veterinarian who has bought the slaughterer's truck and hasn't had time to repaint it. The pigs have turned into the very thing they were initially against, mirroring Orwell's view of the rise of the Soviet Union and its reign of oppression.

BACK TO THE FUTURE

Orwell knew his health might prevent him from completing the novel that contained the messages he really wanted to convey. Dogged by poor health, he still managed to complete the first draft of his final book in 1947. Orwell then spent the first half of 1948 in the hospital, and upon release went to Jura to finalize the manuscript. He was under doctor's orders to work only one hour a day, but he couldn't find a typist to travel to the remote Scottish island, so he typed the final clean copy himself. According to his publisher, Fred Warburg, completing this novel was probably what killed Orwell.

What drove him? In a letter that appeared in *Life* magazine on July 25, 1949, Orwell wrote that, "My novel *Nineteen Eighty-Four* is not intended as an attack on socialism, or on the British Labor party, but as a show up of the perversions to which a centralized economy is liable." (A central authority controls the economy by assigning quantitative production goals and allocating raw materials to various industries. The means of production are publicly, rather than privately, owned; for example, an airplane factory would be owned by everyone rather than by a single company like McDonald Douglas.) He goes on to say that he is not trying to predict a certain future, but rather that "English-speaking races are not innately better than anyone else and that totalitarianism, if not fought against, could triumph anywhere."[1] In the words of his publisher Fredric Warburg: "The moral to be drawn is a simple one: *Don't let it happen. It depends on you.*"[2]

Orwell in the mid-1940s, around the time he was writing *Nineteen Eighty-Four*.

Structure

Nineteen Eighty-Four is divided into three parts and includes an appendix. In Part One, we get to know the main character, Winston Smith, his world (as seen through his eyes), and what drives him.

Part Two, the longest section of the book, anchors Smith in this world. We learn about people who may or may not be unconventional thinkers, like Smith. He has an affair and also attends an underground meeting of other dissatisfied citizens. Embedded in this section are drawn-out political tracts written by an alleged enemy of the state named Emmanuel Goldstein. Interestingly, Orwell's publishers "originally wanted Orwell to delete this material because it stops the action of the narrative."[3]

In Part Three, Smith is accused of crimes against the state and tortured by a man whom he had befriended, assuming that like him, the man was disillusioned and willing to overthrow the state. On the contrary, the man (named O'Brien) is loyal to the state and, given his understanding of Smith, O'Brien knows precisely how to torture him.

Nineteen Eighty-Four concludes with an appendix called "The Principles of Newspeak." This section of the book is Orwell at his literary criticism best: a scholarly explanation of the guiding values for the dystopian world he has just described. In many ways, it is the most important part of the book but again, publishers wanted to cut it, finding it unnecessary.[4]

Plot Summary

Part One

In the first chapter, we're introduced to the novel's main character, Winston Smith. We learn that he is living in a futuristic world in which people are under constant surveillance via something called a telescreen, a device that both receives and transmits data. This world is called Oceania, a "super state" comprised of North and South America, the British Isles, Australasia, and southern Africa—where a totalitarian regime is ruled by one force called Big Brother. In a totalitarian state there is complete government control; citizens cannot express opposition. Though we never ever actually meet him, Big Brother's image is conveyed on posters and the telescreen. When Winston asks an Inner Party member of his acquaintance about Big Brother, he receives no clear answer. In essence, Big Brother is a concept invented by those in power to intimidate citizens and extract their complete loyalty. In the novel, Big Brother serves as Orwell's device for conveying the dangers of an overreaching government.

In this state, there are no individual freedoms. Owning a book or having thoughts that deviate from doctrine are labeled "thoughtcrime," an offense punishable by death. And Winston is about to commit a crime in this futuristic world: keeping a diary. (Though "nothing was illegal, since there were no longer any laws, but if detected it was reasonably certain that it would be punished by death or at least twenty-five years in forced-labor camp."[5]

As the chapter unfolds, we realize that Smith has been disillusioned for some time. Though he works for the Ministry of Truth, we get the sense that his work involves something far from truth. He is not keen on the daily "Two Minutes Hate," a ritual in which a video of Emmanuel Goldstein, supreme enemy of the state, is projected on telescreen throughout Oceania and all ruling Party members are supposed to scream, throw things, and denounce Goldstein. In fact, when the Two Minutes Hate begins, Winston's diaphragm constricts. He cannot see the face of Goldstein "without a painful mixture of emotions and throughout Goldstein's speeches that attack the doctrines of the Party, Winston perceives "an attack so exaggerated and perverse that a child should have been able to see through it." One of the worst things about the Two Minutes Hate, Winston notes, is not that "one was obliged to act a part, but that it was impossible to avoid joining in."[6]

During the Two Minutes Hate, two people whom Winston vaguely recognizes walk into the room. One is a dark-haired woman who sits next to him and gives him "a quick sidelong glance which seemed to pierce right into him and for a moment [fill] him with black terror." Winston briefly considers that she may be part of the Thought Police. The other newcomer is a man called O'Brien. Winston knows O'Brien is part of the Inner Party—an elite group of Oceanic society who are second in command only to Big Brother and who represent only two percent of the population. Despite his standing, Winston suspects, even hopes, that O'Brien feels the way he does. He bases this on the fact that when the Two Minutes Hate meeting breaks up, he and O'Brien look straight at each other for a fraction of a second and "for as long as it took to happen Winston knew—yes he *knew*!—that O'Brien was thinking the same thing as himself . . . 'I am with you,' O'Brien seemed to be saying to him. 'I know precisely what you are feeling. I know all about your contempt, your hatred, your disgust. But don't worry, I am on your side!'"[7]

It may seem implausible that something as fleeting as a moment of staring could convey so much, but in a society where speaking one's true thoughts is impossible, even something as small as a sideways glance can be meaningful. Orwell is exposing what he perceives are the true horrors of a totalitarian government, where people are not allowed to express anything other than slogans, such as WAR IS PEACE,

FREEDOM IS SLAVERY, and IGNORANCE IS STRENGTH. Void of any meaning, people become less unique and isolated from one another.

After his moment with O'Brien, Winston opens the diary and begins to write, taking care to avoid the spying telescreen. He writes DOWN WITH BIG BROTHER, filling half a page, until he's interrupted by knocking at his door. A terrified Winston assumes it is the Thought Police.

Winston opens the door to his neighbor, Mrs. Parsons, whose husband, Tom, works with Winston at the Ministry of

In the 1984 film version of *Nineteen Eighty-Four*, John Hurt portrayed Winston Smith, who dares to question the propaganda that he helps to create in his job at the Ministry of Truth.

Truth. Tom Parsons is described as "a fattish but active man of paralyzing stupidity, a mass of imbecile enthusiasms—one of those completely unquestioning, devoted drudges on whom, more even than on the Thought Police, the stability of the Party depended."[8] Mrs. Parsons has summoned Winston because Tom is not home and the sink is backed up. We learn most people live in less than optimal conditions—old apartments with flaking paint and bursting pipes and inadequate heat. Repairs are mostly done by tenants since anything major must be approved by a committee.

The tenants' plight is reminiscent of the former Soviet Union, where after the revolution the large homes of the ruling class were subdivided into small apartments, with as many as five people crammed into a single room. Author Sheila Fitzpatrick writes, "People lived in communal apartments, usually one family to a room and in dormitories and barracks. A small, highly privileged group had separate apartments. A larger group made their homes in corridors and 'corners' in other people's apartments."[9] Because almost all housing was state property, housing authorities "determined how much space apartment dwellers were entitled to and these space norms—the notorious 'square meters'—were engraved on every big-city-dweller's heart."[10]

Inside the Parsons' apartment, their two children are leaping and shouting, imitating the Thought Police by chanting to Winston "You're a traitor. You're a thought criminal! You're a Eurasian spy!" foreshadowing what is to come for Winston Smith. Back in his own apartment, Winston reflects on the way the Party has made children into spies. "[T]hey were systematically turned into ungovernable little savages, and yet this produced in them no tendency whatever to rebel against the discipline of the Party. On the contrary, they adored the Party and everything connected with it."[11]

A news flash comes across the telescreen proclaiming that Oceania has won a great victory at the Malabar front (South India). Along with this glorious news comes the announcement that as of next week, chocolate rations will be reduced from thirty grams to twenty. The fact that Winston is not surprised at the bad news is an indication that this is a typical ploy of the Party: to announce yet another restriction on the heels of a national triumph.

The chapter ends with Winston reflecting on the nature of the "scared principles of INGSOC" (English Socialism), Newspeak (the official language of the state designed to eliminate words that encourage free thought), doublethink, and "the mutability of the past." He feels utterly alone and knows that in some respects he is going to die because he is different and has dared to think his own thoughts. He has even written in his diary that "thoughtcrime does not entail death: thoughtcrime IS death." And though Winston realizes hiding the diary is futile, he nonetheless marks it with a piece of dust so that he will know if the book is found.[12]

In chapter 3, Winston dreams of his mother, father, and baby sister who disappeared when Winston was ten or eleven. He believes they were taken in government purges. In the dream, he sees his mother holding his sister and though he cannot say why, he feels responsible for their disappearance. The dream moves to the dark-haired girl from the opening chapter and a somewhat erotic image of her tearing off her clothing. To him, this seems like an annihilation of "a whole culture, a whole system of thought, as though Big Brother and the Party and the Thought Police could all be swept into nothingness by a single splendid movement of the arm."[13]

The telescreen shrieks Winston out of bed to do a series of exercises led by a woman on the telescreen. He mechanically performs the exercises, while thinking about his childhood and a time when his country was not at war. But he comes up blank. "You remembered huge events which had quite probably not happened, you remembered the detail of incidents without being able to recapture their atmosphere, and there were long blank periods to which you assign nothing." One thing Winston does remember is that despite the Party line, Oceania had been aligned with Eurasia. He realizes that the Party's power lies in its ability to control people's memories, thereby forcing them to believe whatever it says to be true. He knows too from his work in the Records Department at the Ministry of Truth (altering news articles and documents to suit the party's needs) that this mind control is achieved by systematically removing all references to historical events that do not fit with the Party's current views. In other words, all

WHAT'S IN A NAME?

According to commentator Eugene Goodheart, Orwell may have had a very definite purpose in naming his protagonist Winston Smith. His last name is so common as to make the character seem like an "everyman," while the name Winston, especially in 1949, conjured the image of Britain's great leader, Winston Churchill. Orwell's Winston struggles for freedom, just as Churchill did against Nazi Germany. "In coupling the ordinariness of Smith with the extraordinariness of the British leader, Orwell seems to be suggesting that in the totalitarian society of Oceania the spirt of freedom may reside in the ordinary person," writes Goodheart.[14]

versions of events are purged so that only the current version exists. This is done with everything, including newspapers, books, movies, songs, and even pornography; "from a statue to a slog, from a lyric poem to a biological treatise, and from a child's spelling book to a Newspeak dictionary."[15]

Despite his being a cog in a large machine of deception, Winston enjoys his work because it includes "jobs so difficult and intricate that you could lose yourself in them as in the depths of a mathematical problem—delicate pieces of forgery in which you had nothing to guide you except your knowledge of the principles of Ingsoc and your estimate of what the Party wanted you to say."[16] In a world where there isn't much to enjoy, people find pleasure in an intellectual challenge even when that means doing something that is potentially harmful to other humans.

At lunch, Winston talks with Syme, an acquaintance who is a specialist in Newspeak. Interestingly, "friend" is not really the right word for this relationship: "You did not have friends nowadays, you had comrades; but there were some comrades whose society was pleasanter than that of others." Syme is excited about a project he's working on to update the 11th edition of the Newspeak dictionary. His task is to eliminate words from the language that allow people to express themselves; for example, instead of the words "splendid" and "excellent," the words will be "good," "plusgood," "doubleplusgood," and so on. To Winston, he says with delight, "You don't grasp the beauty of the destruction of words," and "Don't you see that the whole aim of Newspeak is to narrow the range of thought," which of course Winston does see. Here, we learn a bit about "the proles" (the proletariat, or working class), a group of people for whom the rules of the state do not fully apply and who are in Syme's opinion, not even human. In the course of this conversation, it occurs to Winston that Syme will probably be eliminated (or in Orwell's word "vaporized") for being too intelligent, for seeing too clearly and speaking too plainly. "The Party does not like such people," he thinks. His prediction turns out to be true.[17]

Back in his apartment that evening, Winston again writes in his diary. This time, he recalls an evening when he had sex with a prole prostitute. It is also the first time we learn that Winston is married to a woman called Katharine, a woman whom he's dubbed "the human sound track" because she "had not a thought in her head that was not a slogan, and there was no imbecility, absolutely none, that she was not capable of swallowing if the Party handed it out to her."[18] Winston confesses to his diary that having sex with Katharine was unpleasant and that he could have tolerated their marriage except that she kept insisting they produce a child. When they did not, she moved out.

From this reverie, Winston reflects that, "if there is hope, it lies in

In choosing his main character's name, Orwell invokes thoughts of Winston Churchill, Britain's highly regarded prime minister in the 1940s and 1950s.

the proles." As the largest population in Oceania (85 percent), Winston believes that they are the only group with enough critical mass to start a revolution. But, he writes, "Until they become conscious they will never rebel and until after they have rebelled they cannot become conscious," immediately realizing that he sounds just like the Party. The next several paragraphs are an exposé of communist ideology. Through Winston, Orwell describes how the proletariat labored under the burden of capitalism, how the Party liberated them and then oppressed them in its own way. In the novel, Winston notes that this oppression occurs through doublespeak (which the Party uses to teach that the proles are "natural inferiors who must be kept in subjection, like animals by the application of a few simple rules"), using the Thought Police to spread false rumors, and eliminating any who seemed a little too intelligent and capable of causing trouble. None of the strictures of the Party apply to the proles: There is no prohibition on sex, divorce, or religion, and there are no telescreens in their homes because they are beneath consideration.[19]

Winston considers what life may have been like before the revolution and copies a passage from a history textbook he has borrowed from the Parsons into his diary. The text that he copies reads like a political tract: It demonizes capitalists as "fat, ugly men with wicked faces" and describes all of the evil things capitalists did before the Party stopped them. Winston's thoughts wander to three alleged counterrevolutionaries named Jones, Aaronson, and Rutherford. The Party arrested them in the 1960s, they confessed their crimes, and they were released. Winston recalls seeing them at a café and that shortly after that, they were rearrested, confessed to their old crimes as well as new ones, and then executed. Five years after that, Winston came across an article that proved the men were not

THE PROLETARIAT

According to Karl Marx, one of the founders of Communist theory, the term "proletariat" describes "a class of wage workers engaged in industrial production, whose chief source of income is derived from selling their labor."[20] As an economic category it was separate from the poor, the working classes, and the *Lumpenproletariat*.

Because proletariats have a low position in a capitalist society and are subject to the whims of economy and employment, Marxists usually see them as living in poverty. However, according to the Marxist view, the proletariat is not part of the poor class because some members are highly skilled or are non-wealthy entrepreneurs. Though political tracts may blend the proletariat and working class, true Marxists see proletariats as workers who are engaged in industrial production, while "working class" refers to everyone who works for a living, including white collar workers, hired help, and farmers. There is also a class of marginal and unemployable workers called the Lumpenproletariat. This group includes beggars, indigents, and criminals.

guilty of the crimes to which they had confessed. While this revelation was not a surprise to him, it was "a fragment of the abolished past, like a fossil bone which turns up in the wrong stratum and destroys geological theory." In other words, he had proof the Party had lied and that knowledge could "blow the Party to atoms" if only its existence could be widely known. Instead, Winston destroys the fragment in the memory hole.[21]

"I understand HOW: I do not understand WHY," Winston confesses in his diary. He see how the Party works but cannot understand its ultimate goals. He wonders if perhaps he is the crazy one, believing as he does that the past cannot be altered and whether the definition of lunacy is "a minority of one." Winston concludes that he must trust the evidence of his eyes and ears, that "[f]reedom is the freedom to say that two plus two makes four. If that is granted all else follows." In upholding his trust in his own senses, Winston further alienates himself from that which the Party has created.[22]

One spring evening, Winston decides to forego the obligatory ritual of attending communal recreation. He knows it is risky to engage in "ownlife" (Newspeak for "individualism and eccentricity") but the weather is warm, the color of the evening sky is alluring, and the thought of "boring, exhausting games, the lectures, the creaking camaraderie oiled by gin, seemed intolerable."[23] Instead, he walks around a prole neighborhood. Here we learn about those who are considered too insignificant to be in the Party. Their lives appear to be much like they were before the revolution. Proles are allowed pubs, sex, and the lottery, and Winston, believing that any hope for the future lies in proles organizing, tries to speak with them.

Winston finds a man outside a pub and buys him a beer, but the man is too elderly and his thoughts too scattered for Winston to get any information. However, he stumbles upon the junk shop where he bought the diary and speaks with the proprietor, a sixty-year-old man called Charrington. Interestingly, Charrington offers more coherent memories of the past and offers Winston some interesting bits: street and church names and a description of a "farthing." He also takes Winston to an upstairs room from which he is selling furniture. Winston notices that the room is comfortable: It "awakened in him a sort of nostalgia, a sort of ancestral memory. It seemed to him that he knew exactly what it felt like to sit in a room like this."[24] Most significantly, there is no telescreen, and Winston briefly fantasizes about renting the room.

As Winston leaves the shop and the prole neighborhood, he sees the girl with the dark hair. He is convinced that not only has she been following him but that she is an agent of the Thought Police or an amateur spy determined to turn him in. He rushes home and tries to write in his diary. But his thoughts turn to the way the Party captures and tortures non-believers into confessions and then, inevitably, vaporizes them. "To be killed was what you expected. But before death (nobody spoke of such things, yet everybody knew of them) there was the routine of confession that had to be gone through: the groveling on the floor and screaming for mercy, the crack of broken bones, the smashed teeth and the bloody clots of hair... Nobody ever escaped detection, and nobody ever failed to confess."[25]

In this chapter, Orwell takes the idea of the proletariat—the very same concept used in totalitarian ideology—and turns it on its head. Rather than elevate the class of laborers or sing its praises, Orwell shows that the working man is nothing more than a cog in the machinery of the Party. In this way he makes a dig at the hypocrisy he witnessed in Spain during the Civil War and in the in the rise of Soviet Communism.

Part Two

One morning at work, Winston encounters the dark-haired girl face-to-face. She is walking toward him with her arm in a sling when she trips and falls in front of him and secretly slips a note into his hand. Back in his cubicle Winston opens the note, which reads "I love you." He pushes it down the memory hole, but it becomes difficult for him to concentrate on the work he usually finds engaging. His suspicion of the dark-haired girl has been replaced with feelings of longing and lust. Eventually they arrange to meet.

On the appointed day, Winston and the girl meet in a secluded spot in the woods about a half hour from their workplace. The girl kisses Winston and though "she was utterly unresisting," Winston at first cannot think what to do, having been without a woman for so long. He learns that the girl's name is Julia and that she already knows things about him, starting with his name. He discovers that Julia is also disgusted by the Party's dogma and contradictions. Even though she is younger and more physically appealing than he, she is attracted to Winston because she recognizes him as a person "who doesn't belong," who understood the moment she saw

Winston and Julia (Hurt and Suzanna Hamilton) view themselves as outsiders and embark on an intense, dangerous affair.

him that Winston "was against them." Winston's attraction to Julia is not just physical. The act of involving himself with her is "a blow struck against the Party . . . a political act." It is also the first time in the novel Winston appears to have an ally.[26]

A few weeks later, Winston and Julia meet again, and he learns that Julia is twenty-six and spends much of her time attending lectures and demonstrations, leafleting for the Anti-Sex League, and preparing banners for Hate Week. She explains that these activities are camouflage and claims that if one keeps to the smaller rules, the larger ones are easier to break without notice. She lives in a women's hostel, works as a machinist in the Fiction Department, and while not particularly intellectual, she is good with her hands. She also reveals that she worked in the Pornosec division of the Fiction Department, helping to turn out cheap pornography for the Proles, lost her virginity at sixteen, and hates the Party. However, her hatred is rather superficial. For her, life is simple: "You wanted a good time; 'they,' meaning the Party wanted to stop you from having it; you broke the rules as best you could."[27] What seems clear is that Julia has no particular feeling about the Party and its doctrine other than when it intrudes on her personal life; she hates the Party and tells Winston this in no uncertain terms, but she is unconcerned about the larger implications of the Party's ability to control nearly every aspect of life.

At this point, we begin to see important differences between Winston and Julia. The first is ideological. Winston longs for rebellion and imagines that with the help of the Brotherhood (the mythical underground movement led by Oceania's number one enemy and target of Two Minutes Hate, Emanuel Goldstein), change is possible. Julia's approach, on the other hand, is much more superficial. She believes organized rebellion will never work and that living under Party rule is bearable as long as one takes as many liberties against it as possible. The second difference lies in their ages. Though his recollections are vague, Winston can remember a time before the revolution, while Julia cannot. She has grown up with the Party, doesn't believe that the Brotherhood exists, and thinks that wasting time on a rebellion that would inevitably fail is stupid. In her view, "The clever thing was to break the rules and stay alive all the same."[28] Furthermore, Winston's attitude is much more fatalistic than Julia's. Some critics have conjectured that the theme of death is so prevalent in this novel because Orwell was quite ill when writing it, but it is more likely that Orwell was strongly committed to the belief that when one loses compassion and is reduced to cruelty, he might as well be dead.

Compared to Winston, Julia seems buoyant. Though she understands the consequences of betraying the Party, she refuses to feel defeated; "she believed that it was somehow possible to construct a secret world in which you could live as you chose."[29] In setting up this contrast between Winston and Julia, Orwell seems to be saying that without history, one cannot have true perspective.

Julia shares with Winston her theory about the Party's opposition to love and physical closeness. She says, "When you make love you're using up energy; and afterwards you feel happy and don't give a damn for anything. They can't bear you to feel like that." Furthermore, she argues, "If you're happy inside yourself, why should you get excited about Big Brother and the Three-Year Plans and the Two Minutes Hate and all the rest of their bloody rot?" Winston decides to act on his impulse to have sex with Julia and suggests meeting in the room above Mr. Charrington's shop. For his part, Charrington seems to have no problem renting the room. He comments that privacy is a valuable thing and that "[e]veryone wanted a place where they could be alone occasionally" and when they had such a place, it was only common courtesy to keep quiet about it.[30]

Over a period of weeks, they share time together in the room enjoying items from the black market: real sugar, milk, bread, jam, and tea. At one point, Julia puts on makeup and vows to get a dress and heels; "In this room, I'm going to be a real woman, not a Party comrade."[31] During one of their trysts, Winston sees a rat, which sets off a series of nightmarish associations—Winston has an extreme fear of them—foreshadowing what is to come.

Winston and Julia meet as often as possible in Charrington's room. Winston's health has improved, and life seems tolerable even if the pair don't meet every day. What matters is "that room over the junk shop should exist." Yet even as the couple enjoy themselves, they know their situation cannot continue forever. Winston divulges that he has a feeling O'Brien is on their side and that he sometimes has the impulse to walk up to the man and announce, "I'm an enemy of the State. Help me." Julia does not think this would so rash; "She was used to judging people by their faces and it seemed natural to her that Winston should believe O'Brien to be trustworthy on the strength of a single flash of the eyes."[32]

Sure enough, O'Brien stops Winston in the hall at the Ministry with the pretext of wanting to give him the latest copy of the Newspeak dictionary. O'Brien gives Winston his address. On the strength of this interaction, Winston is certain that there is an antigovernment movement and others like him. He also recognizes, this is the beginning of his end; "The end was contained in the beginning. But it was frightening; or more exactly, it was like a foretaste of death, like being a little less alive."[33]

In the next chapter, Winston wakes with tears. He has been dreaming of his mother and his last memory of her. This brings back still other memories of his childhood, which "he must have deliberately pushed out of his consciousness over many years." When he describes the dream to Julia, she totally misses its point. For Winston, it's emblematic of what the Party has done to people: persuading them that impulses and human feeling do not matter, while at the same time giving people no control over their physical circumstances. "When once you were in the grip of the Party, what you felt or did not feel, what you did or refrained from doing, made literally no difference. Whatever happened you vanished, and neither you nor your actions were ever heard from again." For Winston, the really horrific thing is that as recently as two generations ago, people had no idea where the government was taking them. They weren't upset because the Party had not yet begun altering history, and when it did, they were already too brainwashed to notice.[34]

Again Winston thinks of the proles. They hadn't succumbed to inhumane behavior. "They had not become hardened inside. They had held onto the primitive emotions which he himself had to relearn by conscious effort." Winston tells Julia that it is important not to betray each other. It's not about confessing—that cannot be helped, but what is essential is their feelings for one another; in essence the thing that makes them human. Facts could be traced and beaten out of a person, but feelings could not. If you believed that staying human was important, "[t]hey could not alter your feelings; for that matter you could not alter them yourself, even if you wanted to. They could lay bare in the utmost detail everything you had done or said or thought, but the inner heart, whose workings were mysterious even to yourself, remained impregnable."[35]

Finally, Winston and Julia visit O'Brien in his home. It is quite a contrast from the way they live. The flats are larger, the food smells better, O'Brien has a servant, and his apartment has an elevator. Significantly, he can turn the telescreen off. When they arrive, O'Brien is working and though he was invited, Winston feels as though O'Brien is irritated at being disturbed. He also feels panic that he might have made a mistake: "For what evidence had he in reality that O'Brien was any kind of political conspirator?"[36]

Still, Winston confesses that he and Julia are guilty of thoughtcrime and adultery. O'Brien confirms that the Brotherhood exists and Emmanuel Goldstein is alive. O'Brien asks Winston and Julia if they are willing to commit to the Brotherhood's cause; that is, commit murder, betray the state, and do any of a number of things that are crimes against the Party. Answering for them both, Winston says yes. When asked if they are also willing to separate and never see each other again, they say no. O'Brien points out they may be disfigured or changed in a major way, and they still say they will not betray each other.

O'Brien praises them for telling the truth and continues to inform them about the Brotherhood. They will work in the dark, literally and figuratively, since maneuvers are all accomplished at night and agents are never informed of anything but their immediate tasks. As with everything in this novel, there is a penalty: It is inevitable that the Party will capture, torture, and kill them.

Winston is now "gelatinous" with fatigue.[37] Everyone had been preparing for Hate Week—processions, singing, speeches, and military demonstrations all with the intent of creating anger toward Eurasia. Without warning, Oceania and Eurasia are now allies and Eastasia is the enemy. There is no formal announcement; everyone just understands and Hate Week goes on as planned, albeit with a different target. As to the banners and posters with the wrong information, they are the work of Goldstein and his Brotherhood.

Winston is attending a rally in central London when the switch happens and the speaker switches to the current Party line without even a pause. During the chaos at the crowded rally, someone slips Winston a briefcase with a copy of Goldstein's book. Winston can't read the book immediately since he's now required to work overtime to correct documents to match the Party's new version of history. Finally, after working non-stop for six days, Winston goes to the room above Charrington's shop and reads. The book, entitled *The Theory and Practice of Oligarchical Collectivism*, confirms Winston's suspicions about historical events and the Party's manipulation of them. (An oligarchy is a government controlled by a small group of people.)

The book seems to be structured in chapters that refute each of the Party's principles: IGNORANCE IS STRENGTH, WAR IS PEACE, FREEDOM IS SLAVERY. The excerpts in this chapter reveal the political philosophy of the Party, much of which alludes to the philosophies of political theorists such as Marx and Trotsky. The book also serves to confirm Winston's (and our) understanding of the world of Oceania. The three superstates (Oceania, Eurasia, and Eastasia) are essentially indistinguishable, and they are constantly at war with the goal of creating fear. The fruits of human labor are undermined and eventually exhausted so that citizens become increasingly impoverished. The real war is not between the superstates but between the state and its citizens. This is necessary to maintain the social hierarchy and increase productivity and efficiency in the working classes.

Interestingly, after a few paragraphs, Winston stops reading "chiefly in order to appreciate the fact that he *was* reading, in comfort and safety."[38] This small detail underscores the repressive nature of totalitarian government and tallies with actual recollections of those who lived under Stalin in Russia, especially interesting as Orwell died in 1950 and could not have known how oppressive life would become in the USSR. However, it appears he had seen enough to predict it with accuracy.

O'Brien (played in the film by Richard Burton) presents himself as sympathetic to Winston and Julia, but ultimately betrays them.

Goldstein's book excites him. "It said what he would have said, if it had been possible for him to set his scattered thoughts in order. It was the product of a mind similar to his own." When Julia arrives, she is less enthusiastic about the book. As the two fall asleep, Winston finds comfort in the thought that what he has read confirms he is not crazy, that "being in a minority, even a minority of one did not make you mad." At the same time, we know that this book is Winston's death warrant.[39]

Winston and Julia wake to the sound of the "old-fashioned" alarm clock. They watch a prole hanging laundry in the court-yard below and Winston again reflects on the proles and how they may be the salvation for current society. He vows to keep his mind alive and pass on the secret that two plus two makes four. "We are the dead," he says, and Julia repeats this like a mantra. Then a third "iron" voice repeats the phrase. Julia and Winston realize they have been caught. Within moments they are surrounded by "solid men in black uniforms, with iron-shod boot and their feet and truncheons in their hands."[40] They beat Julia and remove her from the room while Winston remains under guard. He wonders if Charrington has also been arrested until he realizes that Charrington is there, minus his prole accent and looking a lot younger (his white hair is now black). He is a member of the Thought Police and has been planning this moment for a long time.

Part Three

The final section of the book is a chronicle of Winston's torture at the hands of the Ministry of Love. As it begins, Winston doesn't know where he is but assumes he is in the Ministry of Love. He is unsure what time of day he was arrested and cannot remember when he last ate. He does remember being put in a cell with proles. A telescreen barks out orders to keep still, take hands out of pockets, and stop talking. Significantly, in prison, the "ordinary" prisoners largely ignore the Party members. It's as if inside the prison the usual social hierarchy has been turned on its head, with the proles and their crimes—theft, prostitution, murder—ranking at the top and the members of the Party who have dared to commit crimes against the state at the bottom.

Winston doesn't think at all about Julia. Though he will not betray her, he "felt no love for her, and he hardly even wondered what was happening to her." Instead, Winston thinks of O'Brien. "O'Brien must know that he had been arrested. The Brotherhood, he had said, never tried to save its members. But there was the razor blade; they would send the razor blade if they could." As his thoughts turn to how he might end his life, Winston is surprised to see Parsons, his next-door neighbor, in the holding cell. Apparently, Parsons had called out "Down with Big Brother" in his sleep and his daughter reported him to the Thought Police.[41]

References are made to Room 101. Winston assumes this is place where torture takes place. At one point a prisoner is called to the room and begs to be left alone. He says he'll turn in anyone, including his entire family if only they will not make him go to Room 101. Winston has the alarming revelation that despite his theories to the contrary, in this prison, "you could not feel anything, except pain and the foreknowledge of pain."[42] At this point we understand that his spirit will be crushed. Just as he has this thought, O'Brien walks into the cell.

Winston assumes O'Brien has also been arrested, but in fact O'Brien has been working for the Party all along, a fact that he insists Winston has always known. Behind O'Brien a guard with a truncheon, or large club, approaches and begins beating Winston, who considers the nature of pain. "Never for any reason on earth could you wish for an increase of pain. Of pain you could wish only one thing: that it should stop. Nothing in the world was so bad as physical pain."[43] Through Winston, Orwell seems to be saying that no matter how idealistic or heroic one would like to be, we as human have limitations and physical discomfort is a way to most people's ethical undoing.

Winston is taken to a room where he is beaten, interrogated, and forced to confess to crimes he has not committed. Winston is strapped into a chair and connected to an electrical device that O'Brien controls. The device also appears to let O'Brien read Winston's mind. O'Brien delivers shocks to Winston every time he refuses to accept O'Brien's viewpoint. For example, O'Brien holds up four fingers and tells Winston that he is holding up five. When Winston becomes confused and insists that he cannot help seeing what is in front of his eyes, that two and two *are* four, O'Brien shocks him and says, "Sometimes Winston. Sometimes they are five. Sometimes they are three. Sometimes they are all of them at once. You must try harder. It is not easy to become sane."[44] We learn that Winston is in the so-called "learning phase" of his total brainwashing. According to O'Brien, Winston is headed to Room 101 not to be punished or tortured but to be "cured." Juxtaposed with Winston's earlier thoughts about humanity being tied to the ability to feel and think for themselves, this scene emphasizes that the Party seeks ultimate control over every citizen.

The next phase of Winston's brainwashing is "understanding." In chapter 3, we learn that the Party wants power for its own sake. There is no interest in creating a utopia. As for others, like the Nazis or Russian Communists, O'Brien acknowledges that they "came very close to us in their methods." But he contends that they were cowards and hypocrites because they refused to acknowledge why they had seized power and believed "that just around the corner there lay a paradise where human beings would be free and equal." Not so here: Power is not a means; it is an end.[45]

O'Brien continues to debase Winston, forcing him to look at his broken body in a mirror, and wrenches out one of Winston's remaining teeth. If Winston's "spirit" is still identifiable, his body is not and it horrifies him enough to give into O'Brien. Still this is not enough. Winston must go through the "acceptance" phase. To underscore the futility of resisting the Party's wishes, O'Brien reminds Winston, "Everyone is cured sooner or later," and "In the end we shall shoot you."[46]

O'Brien knows Winston well and realizes he still feels hate for Big Brother, and if not love, then a bond with Julia. The final step in Winston's cure is to love Big Brother and for this he must go to Room 101. The room is essentially a personalized torture chamber that contains "the worst thing in world," which in Winston's case is rats. He is fitted with a hood into which the rats will be released. O'Brien holds a cage of rats closer and closer to Winston's head. Despite his nearly passing out, Winston has an idea: "There was one and only one way to save himself. He must interpose another human being, the *body* of another human being, between himself and the rats."[47] "Do it to Julia," he shouts, and in that moment Winston's brainwashing is complete. He has given up the last of his humanity. Again, it is a physical threat that forces Winston to compromise his ideals, a reminder from Orwell that pain inflicted on one's body is the hardest kind of pain to bear.

Winston is released back into society, and because he is no longer a threat, he is not monitored. He drinks his Victory gin, plays chess, and causes no problems. By chance, he sees Julia and each confesses that they have betrayed one another. Says Julia, "Sometimes, they threaten you with something—something you can't stand up to, can't even think about. And then you say, 'Don't do it to me, do it to somebody else, do it to so-and-so.' And perhaps you might pretend, afterwards, that it was only a trick and that you just said it to make them stop and really didn't meant. But that isn't true. At the time when it happens you do mean it."[48] She goes on to say that at that moment, all you care about is yourself. Realizing you have come to a moment when self-preservation is your only goal, you cannot feel the same way about the person you were willing to sacrifice; in short, you (in this case, she and Winston) have given everything to Big Brother.

Themes

Freedom and Truth

For Orwell, freedom was impossible without truth, and *Nineteen Eighty-Four* "reflects his conviction that a commitment to "objective truth" was fast disappearing from the world."[49] Yet Orwell never actually defines truth. It is clear what happens without it: people are careful not to express anything different from what they are told, the state controls information about the past, present, and the future, and those who speak out are as ineffectual or insignificant as the old man whom Winston finds in the proletarian quarter outside a bar.

In the same way, *Nineteen Eighty-Four* makes a statement about freedom by its absence. Oceania is a place where every citizen's thoughts are controlled. Anyone with different thoughts is a subversive who can be spied upon and picked up by the Party to be "cured." In short, successful citizens of

Oceania are those stripped of the things that make them individuals and, in some sense, human. As Winston writes in his diary, "Freedom is the freedom to say that two plus two makes four. If that is granted, all else follows."[50]

Utopia vs Totalitarianism

According to Professor Eugene Goodheart, *Nineteen Eighty-Four* gave Orwell a platform from which he could dive deeper into the theme of totalitarianism, and while the Soviet model plays a role, the "novel's conception of totalitarian state is not confined to it."[51] Goodheart goes on to point out that the word "utopia" comes from a Greek word that means "no place" and "good place," and that while many writers and thinkers have upheld the notion of a rational and kind society, utopia has "no existence in the real world."[52] To the contrary, revolutions have distorted the ideals to which they initially subscribed, creating dystopia out of what was supposed to be utopia, turning "the dream into a nightmare."[53]

It comes down to a choice between freedom and happiness. Totalitarian regimes cannot allow individual freedom because it would pose a threat to the regime's complete authority. Orwell recognized this through his character Winston Smith, who after being tortured in the Ministry of Truth reflects that "the choice for mankind lay between freedom and happiness, and that, for the great bulk of mankind, happiness was better."[54] However, giving up freedom usually results in a lack of happiness and sense of security. Before his "cure," Winston is always afraid of being caught for thoughtcrime, always aware that he will be punished for wanting privacy or personal relationships. Afterward, only when he is no longer a threat to the state and is basically a shell of a human being, is he no longer watched.

Patriotism and Nationalism

There is a fine line between patriotism and nationalism, and Orwell walked it carefully. In his 1940 essay "My Country Right or Left," Orwell describes a patriotism that holds together the middle and working class and is both traditional and revolutionary. When World War II began, Orwell was against England's involvement, questioning the motives of politicians as power plays. Once England's security became threatened, Orwell's "old fashioned sense of patriotism—among other

AMERICAN RESPONSE TO COMMUNISM

During the early 1950s, at the height of the Cold War, the United States was no longer on friendly terms with Russia. In fact, there was great fear that Russia would dominate Eastern Europe and threaten democracy in Western Europe as well. The Soviets wanted to maintain control of Eastern Europe, thus diminishing the threat from Germany. Between 1947 and 1948, US aid under the Marshall Plan brought Western European nations under American control, while Russian established itself in Eastern Europe. Between 1948 and 1953, the United States and its European allies formed the North Atlantic Treaty Organization (NATO), a unified military command to fend off any Soviet encroachment in Europe.

In the United States, anticommunist feelings ran high. Senator Joe McCarthy headed the House Un-American Activities Committee (HUAC). The committee vigorously attacked anyone suspected of communist beliefs (in a way not unlike the Party in *Nineteen Eighty-Four*). Before McCarthy was stopped, many careers, particularly in Hollywood, were destroyed and people were pressured to turn in friends and coworkers.

things, made him change his mind about fighting."⁵⁵ He wrote "Patriotism has nothing to do with conservatism. It is devotion to something that is changing but is felt to be mystically the same. To be loyal both to Chamberlain's England and to the England of tomorrow might seem an impossibility, if one did not know it to be an everyday phenomenon. […] When red militias are billeted in the Ritz I shall still feel that the England I was taught to love so long ago and for such different reasons is somehow persisting."⁵⁶ Poet Stephen Spender called Orwell a "radical conservative. What he valued was the old concept of England based on the English countryside,"⁵⁷ where being conservative meant being against change simply for its own sake.

In *Nineteen Eighty-Four* Orwell warns of the dangers of unchecked patriotism. It can easily turn to nationalism and fuel political figures like Hitler, Stalin, and Mao Tse-Tung (though Orwell died before the Chinese Revolution). Just as many Germans worshipped Hitler as an adored father, citizens of Oceania love Big Brother and see him as their protector. Just as in actual totalitarian regimes, the children of Oceania are encouraged to sing patriotic songs, recite slogans, wear a uniform, and spy on their parents. Instead of feeling loyalty to family, the children transfer that feeling to the state.

Style

Orwell uses a third-person, omniscient narrator who clearly focuses on Winston Smith. For example, when describing Smith's interaction with his neighbor's children, the narrator says "Winston raised his hands above his head, but with an uneasy feeling, so vicious was the boy's demeanor, that it was not altogether a game."⁵⁸ We already know that Winston has procured a diary and has written "DOWN WITH BIG

BROTHER" in it, but this detail of Winston's uneasiness cues us in to the fact that the narrator will be giving us insights into Winston's thoughts and feelings. So it is no surprise that a few paragraphs later we learn that nearly all the children of Oceania are horrible savages, made so by Party organizations like Spies that encourage children to be ever vigilant for signs of unorthodoxy.

In this novel (as in most of his writing), Orwell's language is precise. He was well aware of the power of words; in fact, he wrote essays about language and its use (or misuse). In "Why I Write," Orwell says that when he was sixteen, he "suddenly discovered the joy of mere words; i.e. the sounds and associations of words" and that he envisioned writing novels "full

Hitler youth gather at a rally in 1936. The children in *Nineteen Eighty-Four* are taught to value Big Brother above all others, an indoctrination similar to that which was used by the Nazi Party.

of detailed descriptions and arresting similes."[59] But Orwell was not really a novelist. He was more a journalist, and he wrote in what biographer Gordon Bowker refers to as "stylish reportage."[60]

In *Nineteen Eighty-Four*, Orwell was particularly punctilious. He zeroed in on the way totalitarian regimes use language as a mechanism for control. He invented Newspeak, a language based on Standard English. Like all languages it is constantly changing. However, in this world, the Party expunges any words or concepts it deems unacceptable and replaces them with words that it finds acceptable, thus narrowing the range of ideas that can be expressed. In fact, Newspeak is expected to shrink rather than grow into the next millennium. As a consequence, there will be fewer words available to express a unique thought, until the pool of words is so small, they will cease to have meaning. This is precisely what the Party intends. By creating this fictional language and documenting it in an appendix, Orwell drives home the point that language is a powerful device that can be used to mislead people. He has no use for political rhetoric or marketing lingo. These are merely ways to control the unthinking masses, and at least one message seems quite clear: think or be damned.

ORWELL TODAY

Like Shakespeare, Orwell came up with concepts and turns of phrase that are used today. One such coinage is the phrase "cold war," which in essence means a war that does not involve fighting, but a lot of hostility.

In February 1945, Orwell wrote an article in which he "speculated that the American political theorist James Burnham had been right in predicting the dominance of world politics by a small number of superpowers."[1] Orwell goes on to say that, "these vast states will be permanently at war with one another, though it will not necessarily be a very intensive or bloody kind of war."[2] Six months later, writing in *Tribune*, Orwell again refers to Burnham, the "two or three monstrous super-states, each possessed of a weapon by which millions of people can be wiped out in a few seconds" and "the kind of world-view, the kind of beliefs, and the social structure that would probably prevail in a state which was at once *unconquerable* and in a permanent state of 'cold war' with its neighbors."[3] The term was then used in the United States by presidential adviser Bernard Baruch in a speech he gave in 1947.[4]

"That governments might lie as a matter of course and that their citizens might never know what constituted 'the truth' was a possibility that had come to fixate George Orwell," states author Stephen Ingle.[5] It turns out this fixation was

ADVENT OF TELEVISION

In 1936, the BBC began broadcasting regularly scheduled TV programs, and in 1939, television was unveiled to the American public at the World's Fair in New York. Though he could not have known what a dominant force it would become in popular Western culture, Orwell was clearly aware of television's potential as a tool for communication. To wit, in *Nineteen Eighty-Four*, the telescreen broadcasts nonstop propaganda and can spy on its viewers.

Expert John Rodden says that Orwell owes much of his posthumous fame to the television adaptations of *Nineteen Eighty-Four* "that coincided with the birth of nation-wide TV and the rise in the age of celebrity."[6] He goes on to say that without mass media to spread phrases like "Big Brother Is Watching You," and words like "doublethink" and "Newspeak," Orwell would have been an obscure writer interesting only to a certain kind of academic. As it is, Orwell has earned his own adjective—to describe a situation as "Orwellian" is to say that it is tyrannical and soul crushing. Headlines often borrow his imagery: "George Orwell May Have Been Optimistic When Imagining Big Brother" or "Digital DoubleThink: Playing Truth or Dare with Putin, Assad, and ISIS."

not unfounded. Consider for example, the US intelligence contractor Edward Snowden, who revealed the National Security Agency was gathering information about US citizens without their knowledge. Or the case of Julian Assange, who published classified US government documents, or journalist Daniel Ellsberg, who leaked classified information about the Vietnam War. In his book *The War on Leakers*, diplomatic historian Lloyd C. Gardner, like Orwell, asks us to consider "why America has invested so much of its resources, technology, and credibility in a system that all but cries out for loyal Americans to leak its secrets."[7]

Critics have suggested that Orwell is dated because his work does not include many concerns of the twenty-first century: feminism, multiculturalism, postmodernism, and other literary movements that came about after he died. Still, that does not stop Orwell scholars from speculating on what he would think or say about the present century, in what commentator Ben Wattenberg referred to as the "wonderful parlor game: What would Orwell have stood for today?"[8]

A family gathers around the television in the 1950s. Even with the technology as new as it was, Orwell foresaw the television's potential for power in his depiction of the sinister telescreen.

LIFE MIMICS ART?

A story reported by United Press International on February 5, 2015, revealed that the Samsung Smart TV with voice activation feature could transmit personal conversations to a third party. The viewer could control the TV through voice recognition, and the company could get information that the viewer might be unaware of transmitting. The default setting was for the feature to be turned on. The company told customers that they would "need to deactivate the voice recognition and make sure they don't speak when there is a microphone on the screen to prevent their private conversations from being recorded."[9] The article shows an excerpt from Samsung's product brochure alongside a description of the telescreen in *Nineteen Eighty-Four*. Though decades apart, the two are remarkably similar.

Orwell would mostly likely not have been of fan of social media on two counts. First and most obvious is the way privacy can be invaded without one even knowing: websites visited and emails sent can be intercepted by information-gathering services. Second, Orwell would have probably recoiled at texting and tweets as cheapening the richness of the English language. Ironically, Orwell now has his own Facebook page, which is maintained by Penguin Random House.

New Takes on Orwell

There have been radio and film adaptations of many of Orwell's works, including *Coming Up for Air*, *Keep the Aspidistra Flying*, and of course, *Animal Farm* and *1984* (as the work, in a move toward Newspeak, has become known). In 2012, the *Hollywood Reporter* noted that street artist Shepard

Fairey was teaming up with two Hollywood studios to produce a new version of *1984*.

The Headlong Theatre Company of London premiered a stage adaptation of *1984* at the Nottingham Playhouse in 2013. Since then, it has been presented in the United States as well as other countries. Adapted by Duncan Macmillan and Robert Icke, the play gets to what Icke considers the essence of the novel, by including the appendix as part of the dramatization: "It's not just Orwell going: 'Here's some stuff I couldn't crowbar in,' it's a very deliberate formal device that throws everything back on the table and forces you to reconsider the central question of the novel: how do you ever know anything—including where you are, who you are, what you think?"[10]

Orwell continues to be a muse for other writers. In 2015, author Andrew Ervin published a work called *Burning Down Orwell's House*. The main character, Ray Welter, seeks refuge from his fast-paced (and dishonest) life as a Chicago advertising executive by going to the actual house George Orwell rented in Jura. Part comedy, part drama, the novel centers on the core question: "Whether the idea of 'escape' itself is just another manipulation sold to us 'proles' by the very same wired world that engulfs and exhausts us. Take a wild guess what George Orwell would say."[11]

Adaptations of *Animal Farm*

In 1954, a British film studio made *Animal Farm* into an animated film, the first full-length animated production in England. It has been discovered that the US Central Intelligence Agency funded the work and went to great lengths to turn Orwell's novel into "an anti-Soviet polemic. This included a changed ending, one that called on those living under communist rule to revolt."[12] The British and American

As today's televisions become "smarter," there is greater potential for privacy breaches and information gathering of the sort seen in Orwell's novel.

governments had also promoted the book around the world in secret, believing that it would be a warning against the dangers of communism. "Orwell became an icon during the Cold War, in other words, due at least in part to the sort of clandestine state propaganda machines he had railed against."[13] These government actions prompted commentator Karl Cohen to write, "No matter how you feel about [governments] meddling with feature films, it appears their involvement in the making of *Animal Farm* was a successful covert operation and it was kept a secret from the public for almost 50 year."[14]

The novel was again made into a film in 1999, with voice-overs by Kelsey Grammer, Peter Ustinov, and Patrick Stewart, as well as some live-action scenes. It continued the 1954 version's tradition of changing the ending into what one reviewer called an "optimistic turn of its final act, suggesting rebirth following the fall of the regime."[15] The film did not get very good reviews.

Nineteen Eighty-Four in 1984

In 1956, a movie version of Orwell's final novel was directed by Michael Anderson. This film and several TV adaptations were significant in taking Orwell's coinages into the mainstream and making him a "cultural and literary talisman."[16] In the United States, "Studio One" on CBS aired a screen adaptation on September 21, 1953. Almost nine million viewers tuned in, which was a huge number for the time. It did well with the critics, too. Jack Gould of the *New York Times* wrote that the program was "a masterly adaptation that depicted with power, poignancy and terrifying beauty the end result of thought control—the disintegration of the human mind and soul."[17]

Though the US version of the film made no mention of Stalin or the USSR, that reference could not be far from people's minds. In the United States, the Cold War was in full swing and Senator Joe McCarthy's campaign against communism was dominating the news. So, too, was publishing magnate Henry R. Luce (publisher of *Time*, *Fortune*, and *Life* magazines). Luce was pro-American, pro-capitalism, and strongly anticommunist, and his magazines "generally suggested what readers should think with regard to the subjects covered. Luce publications frequently utilized library research materials

Big Brother watches over all in the 1956 film version of *Nineteen Eighty-Four*.

to make stories and articles more complete. Reporters and editors worked together on stories in what was called *group journalism.*"[18] So when *Life* magazine devoted two pages to the TV adaptation in an article called "A 1984 Specter on 1953 Screens," people took notice.

A year later, on December 12, 1954, the BBC aired its own television adaptation of *Nineteen Eighty-Four.* While critics praised the production, a lot of the public did not. Most British TV viewers had not read Orwell, and they were not accustomed to explicit scenes of violence. Many accused Orwell of "having a diseased and depraved mind."[19] In their outrage, the British public succeeded in missing his message while at the same time making him and "Big Brother" household words.

Nineteen Eighty-Four was last made into a movie in 1984. Starring John Hurt, Richard Burton, and Suzanna Hamilton, the movie was a fairly faithful film version of the book, and many moviegoers praised the bleak and gritty film. But some critics felt it had nothing to offer as "entertainment." Gene Siskel complained that the director was too obvious in his portrayal of the book to create film with emotional impact. In his review in the *Chicago Tribune*, he wrote: "Sure it's faithful to the book. And sure, the world of Big Brother and his minions is nasty and demeaning. Yet none of it impacted upon me at the gut level."[20] Siskel's counterpart Roger Ebert, however, disagreed: "The 1954 film version of Orwell's novel turned it into a cautionary, simplistic science-fiction tale. This version penetrates much more deeply into the novel's heart of darkness."[21] It seems that Orwell continues to invite controversy both on the page and on the screen. As one critic pondered Orwell's relevance today, he concluded, "Whether Orwell matters, he clearly still fascinates, stimulates and enrages."[22]

CHRONOLOGY

1903– Eric Blair is born in Motihari, Bengal, on August 25.

1904– With mother and older sister, moves to Oxfordshire, England.

1911–1916– Enrolls at St. Cyprian's private school in Eastborne, England, about sixty miles south of London.

1917–1921– Studies as a King's Scholar at Eton.

1922–1927– Works as officer in the Indian Imperial Police stationed in Burma (Myanmar).

1927–1929– While in England on sick leave, decides to quit the Indian Imperial Police. Embarks on "tramping" expeditions in London and Paris to gather material for writing. Begins what will become *Down and Out in Paris and London* and *Burmese Days*.

1930–1933– Returns to England and teaches at boys' private school in Middlesex, called the Hawthorns; publisher Victor Gollancz prints *Down and Out in Paris and London*; George Orwell appears as Eric Blair's pseudonym.

1934– Harper & Row publishes *Burmese Days*.

1934–1936– Works as part-time bookseller at Booklover's Corner in Hampstead; Orwell lives above the shop. Orwell's second novel, *A Clergyman's Daughter*, is published in 1935; Orwell visits northern England to gather information on unemployment, especially coal miners.

1936– Gollancz publishes Orwell's third novel, *Keep the Aspidistra Flying*; meets Eileen Maud O'Shaughnessy, a student in educational psychology at University College; they are married on June 9; publishes the short story "Shooting an Elephant" in *New Writing* literary magazine.

1936–1937– Travels to Spain to observe the fighting and report on it; joins a militia of the Independent Labor Party,

Partido Obrero de Unificación Marxista (POUM), and fights; serves for 115 days, becoming increasingly disillusioned with the fighting between the left-wing factions.

1937— In May, Orwell is shot in the throat and escapes to France with Eileen; writes of his experiences in *Homage to Catalonia*.

1938–1939— After Gollancz refuses to publish *Homage to Catalonia*, Orwell is released from his obligations to the publisher and Secker & Warburg publishes it instead; travels to Marrakesh with Eileen and writes *Coming Up for Air*.

1940— A collection of three essays entitled *Inside the Whale* is published by Gollancz.

1941–1943— Becomes an employee of the BBC Eastern Service (covering India); resigns two years later to become literary editor of *Tribune*, a weekly left-wing newspaper.

1945— Eileen Blair dies; Secker & Warburg publishes *Animal Farm*.

1946— *Animal Farm* is published in the United States.

1947— Starts his famous essay "Such, Such Were the Joys," excoriating the British middle class and in particular his early days at boarding school; Orwell is hospitalized near Glasgow with tuberculosis.

1948— Leases Barnhill on the remote island of Jura, Scotland; spends five months on Jura, writing *Nineteen Eighty-Four*.

1949— Orwell's health declines; after completing a first draft of *Nineteen Eighty-Four*, Orwell is hospitalized in Gloucestershire, England; moves to University College Hospital, London, in September; marries Sonia Brownell in his hospital room.

1950— Dies on January 21 at the age of forty-six.

CHAPTER NOTES

Chapter 1. "Prose Like a Window Pane"

1. George Orwell, "Why I Write," *The Orwell Reader* (New York: Harcourt, Brace and Co., 1956), p. 390.
2. Ibid.
3. John Rodden, "On George Orwell," *Critical Insights George Orwell* (Ipswich, MA: Salem Press, 2013), p. 3.
4. Orwell, "Why I Write," p. 392.
5. Ibid., p. 396.
6. Ibid.
7. John Rodden, "The "Orwellian" Night of December 12," *Society* 52, no. 2, (April 2015): pp. 159–165.
8. Michael Sheldon, *Orwell: The Authorized Biography* (New York: HarperPerennial, 1991), p. 5.
9. Rodden. "On George Orwell," p. 3.
10. Ibid., p. 161.

Chapter 2. An Age Like His

1. Michael Sheldon, *Orwell: The Authorized Biography* (New York: HarperPerennial, 1991), p. 13.
2. Ibid.
3. George Orwell, "Such, Such Were the Joys," *The Orwell Reader* (San Diego: Harcourt Brace, Jovanovich, 1956), p. 425.
4. Eugenio Biagini, "Great Britain," *Europe 1789-1914: Encyclopedia of the Age of Industry and Empire*, ed. John Merriman and Jay Winter, vol. 2 (Detroit: Charles Scribner's Sons, 2006), pp. 999–1014.
5. Sheldon, p. 75.
6. Orwell, "Such, Such Were the Joys," p. 426.
7. Sheldon, p. 72.

8. Gordon Bowker, *Inside George Orwell: A Biography* (New York: Palgrave McMillan, 2003), p. 57.

9. Denys King-Farlow, E. A. Caroe and George (Dadie) Rylands quoted in Bowker, p. 53.

10. Steven Runciman quoted in Bowker, p. 54.

11. Bowker, p. 57.

12. John Rodden, "On George Orwell," *Critical Insights George Orwell* (Ipswich, MA: Salem Press, 2013), p. 4.

13. Sheldon, p. 135.

14. Ibid., p. 136.

15. Ibid., p. 143.

16. George Orwell, *The Road to Wigan Pier* (New York: Harcourt, Brace and Co., 1958), p. 180.

17. Bowker, p. 104.

18. Ibid.

19. Sheldon, p. 161.

20. Bowker, p. 110.

21. Ibid., p. xiii.

22. George Orwell, *Letter to Eleanor Jacques in Orwell and Angus*, eds., p. 81.

23. Bowker, p. 183.

24. George Orwell, "Review. Herman Melville by Louis Mumford" in Sonia Orwell and Ian Angus, eds., *The Collected Essays, Journalism & Letters of George Orwell, Volume 1* (Harcourt, Brace & World, 1968), p. 19.

25. Ibid., p. 21.

26. Ibid., p. 20.

27. Bowker, p. 134.

28. John Rossi, "Biography of George Orwell," *Critical Insights George Orwell* (Ipswich, MA: Salem Press, 2013), p. 26.

29. "Spanish Civil War," *Compton's by Britannica, v 6.0.* 2009, *eLibrary*, Web (accessed April 29, 2016).

30. "Spanish Civil War," *Europe Since 1914: Encyclopedia of the Age of War and Reconstruction*, ed. John Merriman and Jay Winter, vol. 4 (Detroit: Charles Scribner's Sons, 2006), pp. 2416–2424.

31. George Orwell, *Homage to Catalonia* (Boston, MA: Houghton Mifflin Harcourt, 1980), p. 210.

32. Sheldon, p. 326.

33. Rossi, p. 26.

34. "Spain," *Britannica School,* Encyclopædia Britannica, Inc., 2016, http://school.eb.com/levels/high/article/108580 #70444.toc, (accessed April 24, 2016).

35. Ibid.

36. Rossi, p. 27.

37. Bowker, p. 272.

38. Sheldon, p. 407.

39. Ibid.

40. George Orwell, "Letter to Alex Comfort, Sunday July 11, 1943," in Davidson, Peter, ed., *A Life in Letters* (New York, NY: W.W. Norton, 2013), p. 214.

41. Rossi, p. 28.

42. George Orwell in Anderson, Paul, ed., *Orwell in* Tribune: *"As I Please" and Other Writings 1943–7* (London: Politico's Publishing, Ltd., 2006), p. 161.

43. Ibid.

44. Ibid., p. 162.

45. Ibid.

46. Andrew Means, *George Orwell: An Introduction to the Man*, 2012, e-book, location 152.

47. Sheldon, p. 82.

48. For an example, see Bowker, p. xiii.

49. Rossi, p. 28.

Chapter 3. Autobiographical Journalism

1. John Wain, "Twentieth Century," in Meyers, Jeffrey, ed., *George Orwell* (London: Routledge, 2002), ProQuest ebrary, Web.
2. James Seaton, "Orwell the Essayist and Journalist," *Critical Insights George Orwell* (Ipswich, MA: Salem Press, 2013), p. 134.
3. George Orwell, *Down and Out in Paris and London* (San Diego: Harcourt Brace & Co., 1933), p. 5.
4. Ibid., p. 6.
5. Kermit Lasner, "The Frankfurter and the Hotel," *Kenyon Review* 12.3 (1950): pp. 556–560, Web.
6. Ibid.
7. Orwell, *Down and Out in Paris and London*, p. 17.
8. Lasner, pp. 556–560.
9. Ibid.
10. George Orwell, Introduction to *La Vache enrage*, 1935, in Meyers.
11. Gordon Bowker, *Inside George Orwell: A Biography* (New York: Palgrave McMillan, 2003), p. 180.
12. Ibid., p. 181.
13. George Orwell, *The Road to Wigan Pier* (San Diego: Harcourt Brace & Co., 1958), p. 5.
14. Ibid.
15. Ibid., p. 11.
16. Ibid., p. 13.
17. Ibid., p. 17.
18. Ibid., pp. 34–35.
19. Ibid., p. 156.
20. John Rossi, "Biography of George Orwell," *Critical Insights George Orwell* (Ipswich, MA: Salem Press, 2013), p. 26

21. Ibid.
22. R. R. Kirsch, "The Book Report," *Los Angeles Times* (1923–Current File), August 26, 1958.
23. Sam Leith, "Review: Rereading: A howl of grievance," *Guardian*, February 8, 2014, LexisNexis Academic (accessed April 16, 2016).
24. George Orwell, "Such, Such Were the Joys," *The Orwell Reader* (New York: Harcourt, Brace and Co., 1956), p. 422.
25. Leith.
26. Ibid.
27. Orwell. "Such, Such Were the Joys," p. 435.
28. D. J. Taylor, *Orwell: The Life*, Open Road Media, 2015, E-book Library, p. 58.
29. Taylor quoted in Leith.
30. Taylor, *Orwell: The Life*, p. 59.
31. Ibid.

Chapter 4. Animal Tale

1. Michael Sheldon, *Orwell: The Authorized Biography* (New York: HarperPerennial, 1991), p. 436.
2. Ibid.
3. John Rodden, "Appreciating *Animal Farm* in the New Millennium," *Modern Age* 45.1 (2003): 67+, *Academic OneFile*. Web.
4. George Orwell, "Why I Write," *The Orwell Reader* (San Diego: Harcourt Brace Jovanovich, 1956), p. 392.
5. Rodden, "Appreciating *Animal Farm* in the New Millennium."
6. Sheldon, p. 438.
7. George Orwell, "As I Please 28," in Paul Anderson., ed., *Orwell in Tribune* (London: Politico's Publishing, Ltd., 2006), p. 147.

8. John Rossi, "*Animal Farm*: Beast Fable, Allegory, Satire," *Critical Insights George Orwell* (Ipswich, MA: Salem Press, 2013), p. 152.
9. George Orwell, *Animal Farm* (Boston: Houghton Mifflin Harcourt. 2003), p. 11.
10. Rossi, p. 154.
11. Orwell, *Animal Farm*, p. 41.
12. Ibid., p. 84.
13. Ibid., p. 15.
14. Ibid., p. 3.
15. Ibid., pp. 4, 27.
16. Ibid., pp. 11, 76, 79, 80.
17. Ibid., p. 75.
18. Rossi, p. 162.
19. Orwell, *Animal Farm*, pp. 4, 44.
20. Ibid., p. 4.
21. Ibid., p. 24.
22. Ibid., pp. 4, 29.
23. Ibid., p. 12.
24. Ibid., p. 3.
25. Ibid., pp. 5, 8.
26. Ibid., p. 16.
27. Ibid., p. 22.
28. Ibid., p. 23.
29. Ibid., pp. 23, 24, 27.
30. Ibid., pp. 29–30.
31. Ibid., pp. 33, 36.
32. Ibid., pp. 39, 40.
33. Ibid., p. 43.
34. Ibid., p. 47.
35. Ibid., p. 51.
36. Ibid., p. 49.

37. Ibid., p. 63.
38. Ibid., p. 77.
39. Ibid., p. 79.
40. George Orwell, "Politics and the English Language" in *The Orwell Reader* (San Diego: Harcourt Brace Jovanovich, 1956), p. 355.
41. Orwell, *Animal Farm*, pp. 22, 67.
42. George Orwell, "Literature and Totalitarianism," http://www.orwell.ru/library/articles/totalitarianism/english/e_lat (accessed May 1, 2016).
43. Orwell, *Animal Farm*, p. 58.
44. John Rodden, "Orwell on Religion: The Catholic and Jewish Questions,"*College Literature* 11.1 (1984): pp. 44–58, Web.
45. "Animal Farm," *Novels for Students*, Diane Telgen and Kevin Hile, eds., vol. 3. (Detroit, MI: Gale, 1998), pp. 1–23, *Gale Virtual Reference Library*, Web.
46. Orwell, "Why I Write," p. 394.
47. Orwell, *Animal Farm*, p. 18.
48. Ibid., pp. 82, 84.

Chapter 5. Back to the Future

1. George Orwell, *Life Magazine*, July 25, 1947, pp. 4–6, Google Books Archive, https://books.google.com/books?id=D08EAAAAMBAJ&printsec=frontcover#v=onepage&q&f=false.
2. Fredric Warburg, Press Release, http://www.openculture.com/2014/11/george-orwells-final-warning.html.
3. "Nineteen Eighty-Four," *Novels for Students*, Diane Telgen and Kevin Hile, eds. (Detroit: Gale, 1998), p. 424.
4. Ibid., p. 423.

5. George Orwell, *Nineteen Eighty-Four* (Boston: Houghton Mifflin Harcourt, 2003), p. 94.

6. Ibid., 99, p. 101.

7. Ibid., 97, p. 103.

8. Ibid., pp. 107–108.

9. Sheila Fitzpatrick, *Everyday Stalinism Ordinary Life in Extraordinary Times: Soviet Russia in the 1930s* (New York: Oxford University Press, 1999), p. 46.

10. Ibid.

11. Orwell, *Nineteen Eighty-Four*, p. 110.

12. Ibid., pp. 112, 113.

13. Ibid., p. 116.

14. Eugene Goodheart, "Nightmares of History: Animal Farm and Nineteen Eighty-Four," *Critical Insight: George Orwell* (Ipswich, MA: Salem Press, 2013), p. 183.

15. Orwell, *Nineteen Eighty-Four*, pp. 117, 127.

16. Ibid., p. 128.

17. Ibid., pp. 132, 135, 136, 137.

18. Ibid., p. 149.

19. Ibid., pp. 152, 153.

20. "Proletariat," *Britannica School,* Encyclopædia Britannica, 2016, http://school.eb.com/levels/high/article/61526 (accessed April 6, 2016).

21. Orwell, *Nineteen Eighty-Four*, pp. 155, 160.

22. Ibid., pp. 161, 163.

23. Ibid., p. 164.

24. Ibid., p. 177.

25. Ibid., p. 183.

26. Ibid., pp. 203, 207.

27. Ibid., p. 211.

28. Ibid.

29. Ibid., p. 215.

30. Ibid., pp. 213, 217.
31. Ibid., p. 222.
32. Ibid., pp. 228, 230.
33. Ibid., p. 237.
34. Ibid., pp. 238, 241–242.
35. Ibid., pp. 241–242, 244.
36. Ibid., p. 246.
37. Ibid., p. 255.
38. Ibid., p. 260.
39. Ibid., pp. 276, 293.
40. Ibid., p. 298.
41. Ibid., p. 306.
42. Ibid., p. 315.
43. Ibid., p. 316.
44. Ibid., p. 326.
45. Ibid., p. 338.
46. Ibid., p. 348.
47. Ibid., p. 359.
48. Ibid., p. 365.
49. David Dwan, "Truth and Freedom in Orwell's *Nineteen Eighty-Four*," *Philosophy and Literature* 34.2 (2010): pp. 381-393, Web.
50. Orwell, *Nineteen Eighty-Four*, p. 163.
51. Goodheart, p. 181.
52. Ibid., p. 182
53. Ibid.
54. Orwell, *Nineteen Eighty-Four*, p. 337.
55. Michael Sheldon, *Orwell: The Authorized Biography*, (New York: HarperPerennial, 1991), p. 357.
56. George Orwell, *An Age Like This* (Boston: Godine Books, 1968), pp. 539–540.

57. Stephen Spender in Stephen Wadhams, ed., *Remembering Orwell* (Ontario, Canada: Penguin Books, 1984), p. 106.

58. Orwell, *Nineteen Eighty-Four*, p. 109.

59. George Orwell, "Why I Write," *The Orwell Reader* (San Diego: Harcourt Brace Jovanovich, 1956), p. 391.

60. Gordon Bowker, *Inside George Orwell: A Biography* (New York: Palgrave McMillan, 2003), p. 117.

Chapter 6. Orwell Today

1. James Seaton, "The Historical Background of Orwell's Work" in John Rodden, ed., *Critical Insights: George Orwell* (Ipswich, MA: Salem Press. 2013), p. 54.

2. George Orwell quoted in Seaton, p. 55.

3. George Orwell, "The Atom Bomb and You" in Anderson Paul, ed., *Orwell in* Tribune: *"As I Please" and Other Writings 1943-7* (London: Politico's Publishing, Ltd., 2006), pp. 248–249.

4. "Cold War," *Britannica School,* Encyclopædia Britannica, 2016. Web.

5. Stephen Ingle, "Lies, Damned Lies and Literature: George Orwell and 'The Truth,'" *British Journal of Politics & International Relations* 9: pp. 730–746, Web.

6. John Rodden, "The 'Orwellian' Night of December 12," *Society* 52 (2015): pp. 159–165.Web.

7. Publisher's note from Lloyd Gardiner, *The War on Leakers: National Security and American Democracy, from Eugene v. Debs to Edward Snowden* (New York: The New Press, 2016).

8. Ben Wattenburg, "Orwell's Century," *Think Tank with Ben Wattenberg,* Public Broadcasting System, 2003, transcript, http://www.pbs.org/thinktank/transcript990.html (accessed May 7, 2016).

9. Aileen Graef, "Samsung Smart TVs suspected of recording conversations," United Press International, February 9, 2015, http://www.upi.com/Business_News/2015/02/09/Samsung-Smart-TVs-suspected-of-recording-conversations/6891423479640/.

10. Sam Marlowe, "Robert Icke and Ducan Macmillan's *1984* Gets Right Inside Your Head," February 13, 2014, *Metro News*, http://metro.co.uk/2014/02/13/robert-icke-and-duncan-macmillans-1984-gets-right-inside-your-head-4301854.

11. Maureen Corrigan. "Misadventures and Absurdist Charm Take Root in 'George Orwell's House,'" "Fresh Air," National Public Radio, May 13, 2015, transcript, http://www.npr.org/2015/05/13/406457240/misadventures-and-absurdist-charm-take-root-in-george-orwells-house.

12. Tony Shaw, review of Daniel J. Leab, "Orwell Subverted: The CIA and the Filming of Animal Farm," *Journal of American Studies* 42: p. 2.

13. Karl Cohen, "Friday Review: The Cartoon that Came in From the Cold," March 7, 2003, *The Guardian* (London), LexisNexis Academic.

14. Ibid.

15. David Rooney, "Animal Farm," *Variety*, LexisNexis Academic, Web.

16. Rodden, pp. 159–165.

17. Jack Gold, "Television in review: Orwell's '1984,'" *New York Times* (1923–Current File), September 23, 1953, Web.

18. "Henry R. Luce," *Britannica Academic*, Encyclopædia Britannica, Inc., 2016. Web.

19. Rodden, pp. 159–165.

20. Gene Siskel. "Faithful Film Looks Good, but Lacks Bite," *Chicago Tribune* (1963–Current file), February 1, 1985, *ProQuest*, Web.

21. Roger Ebert, "Reviews: 1984," February 1, 1985, RogerEbert .com, http://www.rogerebert.com/reviews/1984-1984 RogerEbert.com.

22. Geoffrey Wheatcroft, "Why George Orwell Is as Relevant Today as Ever," *Guardian*, August 24, 2012, http://www. theguardian.com/commentisfree/2012/aug/24/george-orwell-relevant-today-eve.

LITERARY TERMS

aesthetic—Perception of beauty.

allegory—A story in which characters and events are symbolic of real life and events.

fable—A brief tale with a moral or lesson.

foreshadow—A literary device used to suggest events that may be coming.

irony—The use of words to convey a meaning that is opposite of its usual meaning.

pseudonym—A name taken that is not one's own; an alias.

satire—A way of using humor or sarcasm to ridicule human weakness or foolishness.

Major Works by
George Orwell

Fiction

Down and Out in Paris and London, 1933
Burmese Days, 1934
Keep the Aspidistra Flying, 1936
Coming Up for Air, 1939
Animal Farm, 1945
Nineteen Eighty-Four, 1949

Plays

A Clergyman's Daughter, 1935

Nonfiction

The Road to Wigan Pier, 1937
Homage to Catalonia, 1938
Inside the Whale and Other Essays, 1940
The Lion and the Unicorn: Socialism and English Genius, 1941
Critical Essays, 1946
Shooting an Elephant and Other Essays, 1950
Such, Such Were the Joys (posthumously), *1953*
Collected Essays, Journalism, and Letters of George Orwell, 1968 (4 volumes)

Further Reading

Brunsdale, Mitzi. *Student Companion to George Orwell*. Westport, CT: Greenwood Press, 2000.

Meyers, Jeffrey. *Orwell: Life and Art*. Urbana, IL: University of Illinois Press, 2010.

Orwell, George. *The Orwell Reader*. New York, NY: Harcourt, Brace and Company, 1956.

Sheldon, Michael. *Orwell: The Authorized Biography*. New York, NY: Harper Perennial, 1991.

Websites

George Orwell (1903–1950)
www.orwell.ru/home.html
Includes biographical information as well as faithful replications of many of Orwell's essays, reviews, and articles.

George Orwell at the BBC
www.bbc.co.uk/blogs/radio4/2009/06/the_george_orwell_archive.html
Maintained by the BBC, this site contains information and documents related to Orwell's time at the BBC, as well current interpretations of his work.

New Yorker: Orwell and Son
www.newyorker.com/news/george-packer/orwell-and-son
An account of Richard, the adopted son of Eric Blair and his first wife, Eileen.

INDEX

group journalism, 108

H

Hamilton, Suzanna, 108
"Hanging, A," 16
Harrow, 13
Headlong Theatre Company, 104
Hitler, Adolf, 41, 44, 48, 97
Hollywood, 96, 103, 104
Hollywood Reporter, 103
Homage to Catalonia, 23–24
House Un-American Activities
    Committee (HUAC), 96
Hurt, John, 108

I

Icke, Robert, 104
Indian Civil Service, 15
Ingle, Stephen, 100
Inside the Whale, 24
International Brigades, 21
International Labor Party, 34
irony, 27, 65, 66
ISIS, 101

J

Joyce, James, 17

K

Keep the Aspidistra Flying, 103

L

Left Wing Book Club, 19
Leith, Sam, 36, 37
Lenin, Vladimir, 42
Life, 67, 106
Limouzin, Ida Mabel, 10, 13
Lion and the Unicorn, The, 25
"Literature and Totalitarianism," 62
"London Letters," 24
Luce, Henry R., 106

M

Macmillan, Duncan, 104
Mao Tse-Tung, 97
Marshall Plan, 96
Marx, Karl, 46, 51, 63, 79, 88
*Matrimonial Post and Fashionable
    Marriage Advertiser*, 26
Mayakovsky, Vladimir, 50–51
McCarthy, Joe, 96, 106
Melville, Herman, 17, 19
Mercador, Ramon, 44
Miller, Henry, 24
Mumford, Louis, 17, 19
Mussolini, Benito, 23
"My Country Right or Left," 96

N

National Security Agency, 101
National Unemployed Workers
    Union, 34
Nazi-Soviet Nonaggression Pact, 48
Nazis, 41, 48, 62, 75
New York Times, 106
Newspeak, 74, 76, 80, 99, 101, 103
Nicholas II, 42, 48
"1984 Specter on 1953 Screens,
    A," 108
Nineteen Eighty-Four, 7, 9, 19, 29,
    37, 42, 45, 67–99, 101, 103, 104,
    106–108
North Atlantic Treaty Organization
    (NATO), 96
Nottingham Playhouse, 104

O

omniscient narration, 64, 97
opium trade, 10, 12
Orwell, George,
    early life and career, 10–19,
        21–27
    finding literary success, 27–29